PROPHETS

PRIESTHOOD KEYS

SUCCESSION

HOYT W. BREWSTER, JR.

Deseret Book Company
Salt Lake City, Utah

Library of Congress Cataloging-in-Publication Data

Brewster, Hoyt W.
    Prophets, priesthood keys, and succession / Hoyt W. Brewster, Jr.
      p. cm.
    Includes bibliographical references and index.
    ISBN 0-87579-560-9
    1. Prophets (Mormon theology) 2. Council of the Twelve Apostles
(Church of Jesus Christ of Latter-day Saints) 3. Mormon Church—
Apostles. I. Title.
BX8643.P7B74 1991
262'.1—dc20   91-32110
                                                  CIP

Printed in the United States of America

10   9   8   7   6   5   4   3   2   1

To all who desire to follow
Jesus Christ and
his apostles and prophets

"The arm of the Lord shall be revealed; and the day cometh that they who will not hear the voice of the Lord, neither the voice of his servants, neither give heed to the words of the prophets and apostles, shall be cut off from among the people."

Doctrine and Covenants 1:14

"What I the Lord have spoken, I have spoken, and I excuse not myself; and though the heavens and the earth pass away, my word shall not pass away, but shall all be fulfilled, whether by mine own voice or by the voice of my servants, it is the same."

Doctrine and Covenants 1:38

Contents

Introduction

Prophets Speak to You Personally

In congregations throughout the world and in many languages, Latter-day Saints sing with great enthusiasm, "We thank thee, O God, for a prophet to guide us in these latter days." (*Hymns,* 1985, no. 19.) While William Fowler originally wrote this hymn in honor of the first prophet of this latter-day dispensation of times, it is now traditionally sung in recognition of the *living* prophet — the man whom millions sustain as the President of The Church of Jesus Christ of Latter-day Saints.

The world, in general, is unaware that God has placed a living prophet on the earth today. On the other hand, there are many Latter-day Saints who, though they profess their gratitude for a living prophet in song and testimony, often take lightly the words of counsel proferred by that prophet.

I recall hearing the story of two missionaries who engaged a non-Mormon in a conversation about religion. The discussion led to the topic of prophets, and the two missionaries fervently testified that God had called a living prophet in our day.

"Do you mean to tell me," inquired the man, "that there is a prophet of God on the earth today?"

"Yes, sir!" they replied.

"How does he communicate God's will?" asked the inquirer, who was now very interested.

"Well," one of the missionaries responded, "he speaks at conference, and he writes regular articles in our Church magazines."

With budding curiosity, the man asked, "What did this prophet say most recently?"

There was a moment of uncomfortable silence as each missionary looked hopefully at the other for an answer to the man's question. Finally, they slowly shrugged their shoulders in embarrassment. In subdued voices, they admitted their ignorance. "We haven't read his articles lately," one said. "You see, we've been so busy . . . "

How can one who professes to believe in a living prophet be "too busy" to listen to or read his words? Is the prophet just an administrative head of the Church, or does he really speak the mind and will of God?

How important is the Lord's prophet to you personally? Beyond the fact that he holds the keys of priesthood authority that authorize the saving covenants and ordinances of the gospel that will affect your eternal life, what difference does, or should, a living prophet make in your day-to-day life?

Elder Boyd K. Packer has reminded us that prophets give "quiet counsel on ordinary things which, if followed, will protect us." ("The Gospel—The Foundation for Our Career," *Ensign*, May 1982, p. 85.) Listening to and following the counsel given by the Lord's prophets does make a difference!

Having a personal testimony that God has called prophets to lead us in our day is important. It is vital that every man, woman, and child on this earth come to that knowledge and that they be able to discern between true prophets, who bear the mantle of authority from God, and the pretenders, who falsely profess to have such authority. One of the purposes of this volume is to help seekers after truth come to this understanding.

Salvation Depends on Following God's Prophets

With the death of each prophet, or President of The Church of Jesus Christ of Latter-day Saints, there is some speculation by the uninformed or the misinformed regarding the order of succession and governance in the Church. In recent years, the question has even been raised about who should govern or preside in the Church should the designated leader be disabled.

In addition, there have always been false prophets and self-proclaimed would-be leaders who have raised their voices in opposition to the Lord's servants and sought to establish their own claim to presiding authority. Some have received a great deal of notoriety while others are hardly known beyond the local pastures in which they have preyed upon the flock. Nevertheless, each lamb or sheep led astray is a tragic loss to the Lord and His church.

One's eternal salvation depends upon the ability to recognize and know the true servants of God—those who are authorized to preach His gospel and administer the sacred and saving ordinances thereof. During His mortal ministry, the Savior proclaimed, "He that receiveth a prophet in the name of a prophet shall receive a prophet's reward." (Matt. 10:41.) One must be certain that the prophet he or she is following is a true prophet of God, appointed by Him to the ministry.

The Lord Appoints His Prophets

In these latter days, the Lord declared: "If my people will hearken unto my voice, and unto the voice of my *servants whom I have appointed* to lead my people, behold, verily I say unto you, they shall not be moved out of their place. But if they will not hearken to my voice, nor unto the voice of these *men whom I have appointed,* they shall not be blest." (D&C 124:45–46; italics added.)

We are reminded of the Lord's proclamation to the apostles who served with him during his earthly sojourn: *"Ye have not chosen me, but I have chosen you, and ordained you,* that ye should go and bring forth fruit, and that your fruit should remain: that whatsoever ye shall ask of the Father in my name, he may give it you."* (John 15:16; italics added.)

Men do not seek office in the Church. President J. Reuben Clark, Jr., reminded us that "Church-men do not seek Church office. The best evidence that a man is unfit for Church office is the fact that he wants it." (In Conference Report, Apr. 1940, p. 72.)

We May Know Principles but Not Necessarily Specifics

Clearly God calls His servants. But how does one recognize the true servant of God, the rightful leader of His church? One of the purposes of this volume is to identify those principles that govern the selection of those whom the Lord calls and appoints to lead His people. Regarding this matter, President Spencer W. Kimball observed: "The pattern divine allows for no errors, no conflicts, no ambitions, no ulterior motives. The Lord has reserved for himself the calling of his leaders over his Church. It is a study of great interest and importance." (In Conference Report, Oct. 1972, p. 28.)

Although general principles of the divine pattern of succession will be outlined in this volume, the reader is cautioned against drawing wrong conclusions or assuming to know specifics that have not been revealed. For example, one of the main principles outlined in this volume is that the senior apostle is the presiding officer in the Church. While at any given time we may know the order of apostolic seniority, it does not follow that the particular man next in seniority will someday lead the Church. The Lord regulates this matter. President Spencer W. Kimball said that the Lord "permits to come to the first place only the one who is destined to take that leadership. Death and life become the controlling factors." (In Conference Report, Oct. 1972, p. 29.)

Who will be the next prophet and President of the Church? Generally only the Lord knows. With a few notable exceptions, when He has revealed that knowledge to trusted individuals, the Lord has kept that information to Himself. Thus, we do not presume to know the names of the men foreordained to rise to the position of senior apostle and to receive the mantle of leadership with its accompanying keys of the priesthood.

President Harold B. Lee cautioned against speculation: "Those who try to guess ahead of time as to who is going to be the next President of the Church are just gambling as they might be on a horse race, because only the Lord has the time table. . . . The Lord only knows, and for us to speculate or to presume is not pleasing in the sight of the Lord." ("Admonitions for the Priesthood of God," *Ensign*, Jan. 1973, p. 107.)

Perhaps the bottom-line statement regarding how the Lord selects the prophet and President of the Church is found in the following statement from President Lee: "To those who ask the question: How is the President of the Church chosen or elected? the correct and simple answer should be a quotation of the fifth Article of Faith: 'We believe that a man must be called of God, by prophecy, and by the laying on of hands, by those who are in authority to preach the Gospel and administer in the ordinances thereof.' " ("The Day in Which We Live," *Improvement Era*, June 1970, p. 28.)

Chapter 1

The Role of Prophets
Anciently and Today

God Speaks through Prophets

From the time God conferred keys of priesthood authority on the patriarch of our race — Father Adam — mankind has been tutored by men with special callings. We call these men prophets.

A prophet serves as God's messenger, receiving revelation and making known Deity's divine will. While all righteous men and women have the right to receive revelation regarding themselves or things over which they exercise a stewardship, God has chosen prophets through whom He reveals his will to his disciples, to nations and peoples, or to mankind in general. One of these ancient prophets tells us, "Surely the Lord God will do nothing, *until* he revealeth the secret unto his servants the prophets." (JST, Amos 3:7; italics added.)

Because of the rebelliousness of His children, God has at times in earth's history removed His prophets or His holy priesthood from among the people. For example, ancient Israel lost the powers of godliness associated with the higher priesthood when Moses and "the priesthood which is after the holiest order of God" were taken from their midst because of Israel's hard-heartedness. (D&C 84:18–26.)

Occasionally the prophets have remained among rebellious or unreceptive people but have been forbidden to preach to them. "I did endeavor to preach unto this people," said one of God's ancient servants, "but my mouth was shut, and I was forbidden that I should preach unto them; for behold they had wilfully rebelled against their God." (Morm. 1:16.)

Under such conditions, the illuminating rays of revelation are restricted, and the rebellious are left to grope in the ensuing spiritual darkness. An Old Testament prophet foretold of at least one such period: "The days come, saith the Lord God, that I will send a famine in the land, not a famine of bread, nor a thirst for water, but of hearing the words of the Lord: and they shall wander from sea to sea, and from the north even to the east, they shall run to and fro to seek the word of the Lord, and shall not find it." (Amos 8:11–12.)

One extended famine, a period without prophets, existed on the earth from essentially the time when the last of the biblical apostles of Jesus Christ were taken from among men until early in the nineteenth century. While it is true that the Apostle John (see John 21:20–23; D&C 7) and other chosen servants of God (see 3 Ne. 28:4–9) remained on the earth to continue their ministry, their work was limited. For nearly two millennia mankind in general was deprived of the blessings that come from priesthood and prophets.

A Latter-day Prophet Is Raised Up

Then one spring morning in 1820, the darkness dispersed as the heavens opened and mortal man once again heard the voice of God. A fourteen-year-old boy bearing the name of the ancient prophet *Joseph* (see JST, Gen. 50:25–33; 2 Ne.

3:6–15) was called of God to be the prophet of the Restoration (see JS – H 1:13–20). Just as his illustrious ancestor had risen from the chains of slavery and the darkness of a prison dungeon to save ancient Israel from physical starvation, this modern-day Joseph would throw off the shackles that bound men in spiritual darkness and offer modern-day Israel the chance to be saved from spiritual starvation.

In a later revelation given to this prophet of the latter days, the Lord announced to the world: "Wherefore, I the Lord, knowing the calamity which should come upon the inhabitants of the earth, called upon my servant Joseph Smith, Jun., and spake unto him from heaven, and gave him commandments." (D&C 1:17.) From the spring of 1820 through March of 1830, the young prophet was tutored by revelation and by heavenly messengers sent from God's presence. (See D&C 2–19; JS – H 1:27–75.) Priesthood keys were restored (see D&C 13:1; 27:8–9, 12–13), and additional scripture – the word of God – was made available to mankind.

On April 6, 1830, the Lord Jesus Christ once again established His earthly kingdom among men through the organization of The Church of Jesus Christ of Latter-day Saints, which He declared was "the only true and living church upon the face of the whole earth." (D&C 1:30.) During the next fourteen years of his life, Joseph Smith would continue to receive revelation and declare the mind and will of God to mankind. Additional keys of priesthood authority were received (see D&C 110:11–16), and the fullness of the gospel, including all of the covenants and ordinances of salvation, were once again available to mankind.

With the death of the Prophet Joseph Smith in 1844, the mantle of authority fell upon another prophet called of God. To this day, the keys of priesthood authority have continued in an unending succession of prophets. Each succeeding prophet has been called of God through a divinely established pattern, consistent with the following statement of belief outlined by the first prophet of this last dispensation: "We believe that a man must be called of God, by prophecy, and by the laying on of hands by those who are in authority, to preach the Gospel and administer in the ordinances thereof." (A of F 1:5.)

Prophets Are Foreordained

Prophets are not chosen by chance. The circumstances of time, place, popularity, or association are not what bring them to their callings. Each was foreknown of God and foreordained to his calling long before he began his sojourn on earth. God said to the prophet Jeremiah: "Before I formed thee in the belly I knew thee; and before thou camest forth out of the womb I sanctified thee, and I ordained thee a prophet unto the nations." (Jer. 1:5.)

The prophet Abraham was shown in vision "the intelligences that were organized before the world was; and among all these there were many of the noble and great ones; and God saw these souls that they were good, and he stood in the midst of them, and he said: These I will make my rulers; for he stood among those that were spirits, and he saw that they were good; and he said unto me: Abraham, thou art one of them; thou wast chosen before thou wast born." (Abr. 3:22–23.)

The Prophet Joseph Smith stated: "Every man who has a calling to minister to the inhabitants of the world was ordained to that very purpose in the Grand Council of heaven before this world was. I suppose that I was ordained to this very office in that Grand Council." (*History of the Church,* 6:364.)

Each prophet is sent to earth at the predetermined time God has set for that particular prophet's training and ministry. There is no happenchance in this divine process. The

Lord knows whom He wants to serve, when He wants him to serve, where He wants him to serve, and what He wants him to accomplish.

The prophets are responsible for carrying out God's will. Our responsibility is threefold: to know who God's prophet is, to gain our own witness of his divine calling, and then to follow the counsel he gives. Prophets speak with the voice and authority of God. The Lord has said: "Whether by mine own voice or by the voice of my servants, it is the same." (D&C 1:38.)

What Do Prophets Teach?

Prophets have long been famous for foretelling or prophesying future events. For example, Joseph's rise to power and prominence in ancient Egypt directly resulted from his prophecy of the seven years of abundance to be followed by seven years of famine. (See Gen. 41.) Joseph later prophesied of men and events that would help shape the history and destiny of the House of Israel and of mankind in general. (See JST, Gen. 50:24–36.) Other prophets like Daniel, Ezekiel, Isaiah, and John the Revelator are also well known for foretelling future events. This is the role in which the world generally views a prophet.

As a rule, however, a prophet is more of a *forthteller* than a *foreteller*. (See "Prophet," BD.) In other words, he spends more time teaching principles of righteousness, administering and authorizing ordinances of salvation, and preaching repentance (forthtelling) than he does predicting the future (foretelling).

Because many misunderstand the role of a prophet, they miss much of the important counsel on day-to-day matters that comes from these inspired servants of God. Some even lightly dismiss a prophet's counsel because they consider it insignificant or even foolishness. (See 1 Cor. 2:14.)

Do you recall the Old Testament story of Naaman? He was the "captain of the host of the king of Syria, was a great man with his master, . . . [and] was also a mighty man in valour, but he was a leper." (2 Kgs. 5:1.) Naaman sought to be healed by the word, or under the hands, of the prophet Elisha. He was disappointed and angry when the prophet failed to personally come to him but instead sent a servant to Naaman with instructions to have the leprous man cleanse himself by washing seven times in the Jordan River.

Fortunately, Naaman had some caring servants of his own who convinced their recalcitrant master to follow the prophet's counsel. "If the prophet had bid thee do some great thing," they asked, "wouldest thou not have done it? how much rather then, when he saith to thee, Wash, and be clean?" (2 Kgs. 5:13.) Following their counsel, Naaman humbled himself and did as instructed by the prophet, and he was healed of his malady.

In 1982, citing counsel given by the prophet of the Lord who then stood on the earth, Elder Boyd K. Packer related a modern-day illustration of this story:

> Human nature hasn't changed over the years. Even today some of us expect to be bidden to do some "great things" in order to receive the blessings of the Lord. When we receive ordinary counsel on ordinary things, there is disappointment, and, like Naaman, we turn away.

> Let me give you a modern-day example. President Kimball has been President of the Church for eight years. In virtually every conference sermon he has included at least a sentence telling us to clean up, paint up, and fix up our property. Many of us have paid little attention to the counsel.

> Question: Why would a prophet tell us to do that? Has he no great prophecies to utter?

But, is that not a form of prophecy? For has he not said to us over and over again, "Take good care of your material possessions, for the day will come when they will be difficult, if not impossible, to replace."

Already there is a fulfillment. Families who might have afforded a home when first he spoke now despair of getting one.

For some reason, we expect to hear . . . some ominous great predictions of calamities to come. Instead, we hear quiet counsel on ordinary things which, if followed, will protect us in times of great calamity. ("The Gospel," p. 85.)

There Is Safety in Following Prophets

Is an impending calamity needed for you to turn your ears, your eyes, and your heart to the words of counsel from God's prophet? During the 1990–91 crisis in the Persian Gulf, book stores were besieged by frantic people eagerly seeking information about the last days, Armageddon, prophecy, and anything that would shed light on the unfolding events in the Middle East, or looking for comfort to troubled hearts regarding the dangerous days at hand.

At the height of the hostilities, when the forecasters of doom predicted long-term economic hardships, including shortages of food and energy, there were many who wished they had listened to a prophet's counsel. As recently as April of 1988, the Lord's prophet, President Ezra Taft Benson, had asked: "Are each of us and our families following, where permitted, the long-standing counsel to have sufficient food, clothing, and, where possible, fuel on hand to last at least one year?" ("Come unto Christ, and Be Perfected in Him," *Ensign*, May 1988, p. 85.)

Because of the unparalleled shortness of the ground war, which lasted only one hundred hours until a cease-fire was declared, most people outside the war-torn area did not have to draw upon their reserve supplies of food, clothing, fuel, or savings. However, there were notable exceptions, such as the families whose main provider had been called up to serve in the military during the crisis and who consequently experienced economic difficulties because their normal income had been substantially reduced.

While most families did not have to draw upon such reserves, what about the next time world or local circumstances create such a need? And what about the many who are presently or someday will be underemployed or without work? Consider the advantage a family has that has prepared for such an emergency over one that has not.

Although the war with Iraq was brought to a quick and successful conclusion, we should develop a great hunger and thirst for a knowledge of God's words and ways and a recognition that there is safety in following the counsel of His prophets. President Harold B. Lee once reminded the Latter-day Saints that "the only safety we have as members of this Church is to do exactly what the Lord said to the Church in that day when the Church was organized. We must learn to give heed to the words and commandments that the Lord shall give through his prophet." (In Conference Report, Oct. 1970, p. 152; see also D&C 21:4–5.)

The Testimony of Jesus

The most significant message one could hear — one that would bring great inner peace and comfort not only in times of turmoil and calamity, but also in every day of our lives — is the testimony that we are God's children, that He lives, that He loves us, and that His Beloved Son is our Savior. The supernal calling of a prophet is to bear witness of these things.

Prophets today hold the holy apostolic office. This entails the responsibility to bear witness that Jesus is the Christ, meaning the Messiah or the Anointed One. Jesus Christ is the Savior of mankind. Prophets are *"special witnesses* of the name of Christ in all the world." (D&C 107:23; italics added.)

Anciently, the Apostle John declared that "The testimony of Jesus is the spirit of prophecy." (Rev. 19:10.) This was reiterated by a modern-day apostle and prophet of God. The Prophet Joseph Smith said: "Salvation cannot come without revelation; it is in vain for anyone to minister without it. No man is a minister of Jesus Christ without being a Prophet. No man can be a minister of Jesus Christ except he has the testimony of Jesus; and this is the spirit of prophecy." (*Teachings of the Prophet Joseph Smith,* comp. Joseph Fielding Smith [Salt Lake City: Deseret Book, 1938], p. 160.)

In this sense, then, all men and women should be prophets, possessing the spirit of prophecy. Each one should be endowed with the witness that will bring ultimate salvation, if the individual, through that testimony, receives the saving covenants and ordinances and endures in obedience to the end.

Moses understood the importance of having multiple witnesses of sacred things. He was instructed to select seventy men besides himself upon whom the Lord could send His Spirit. And "when the spirit rested upon them, they prophesied, and did not cease." (Num. 11:25.) When the Spirit also came upon two others (who were not among the original seventy) and they began to prophesy, some in the camp of Israel began to complain. "Forbid them to prophesy," these murmurers said. Perhaps they were thinking, "Let's keep the original seventy as an exclusive group and not allow others to have this special gift."

Moses responded by saying, "Enviest thou for my sake? would God that all the Lord's people were prophets, and that the Lord would put his spirit upon them!" (Num. 11:29.)

What a marvelous message! All men and women should have the spirit of prophecy in bearing witness of divine truths, foremost of which is that Jesus *is* the Christ. Thus, while God selects a specific individual to serve as His official mouthpiece on earth — His prophet, seer, and revelator, and the *one* upon whom He bestows the *keys* of the priesthood — God gives *all* mankind the opportunity to receive the testimony of Jesus and to share that witness with others as the Spirit directs.

The challenge of all men, women, and children throughout the world is to obtain the testimony of Jesus and also the witness of the Spirit that a prophet lives on earth today. Members of The Church of Jesus Christ of Latter-day Saints bear witness to the world that Jesus is the Christ and the Son of God. He has established His church upon the earth and called a prophet to lead it. This prophet serves as the President of Christ's church, but Jesus himself is the head of His earthly kingdom. This knowledge is of the utmost importance to all mankind. For if what we say is true, and we testify that it is, then only within this church will one find the *fullness* of the saving principles and ordinances of the gospel.

Knowing the process whereby God's prophet is called is also vital, for there are many false prophets who would lead astray whomever they can. A major purpose of this book is to bear witness that a true prophet of the Lord lives on the earth today and to identify the inspired process whereby he is called to serve and to govern the affairs of God's church and kingdom on earth.

Chapter 2

Line upon Line: Keys of the Priesthood Restored

The Certainty of a Prophet's Vision

When fourteen-year-old Joseph Smith emerged from the sacred grove that spring morning in 1820, where he had stood in the presence of Deity, he was no doubt filled with wonder and amazement at his singular experience. He had seen what few mortal men have witnessed: God the eternal Father and His holy Son Jesus Christ had appeared to him, and he had heard their voices.

There was absolute conviction in his soul of the reality of their existence: "I had beheld a vision," said the young prophet. "I had actually seen a light, and in the midst of that light I saw two Personages, and they did in reality speak to me." (JS-H 1:24–25.)

Joseph Smith recorded only a few of the instructions he received from these holy beings on that occasion, indicating that he was told "many other things" that he did not record for public eyes. (JS-H 1:20.) Other prophets have similarly limited their sharing of sacred writings and experiences. (See John 21:25; 1 Ne. 14:28; 2 Ne. 4:25; 3 Ne. 26:11, 18; Ether 13:13.)

To our knowledge, Joseph Smith did not receive any keys of priesthood authority on the occasion of this great theophany. These were yet to be restored according to the timetable of the Lord. First there had to be a period of preparation for the budding prophet.

The Prophet's Mission Begins to Unfold

For three and one-half years, the youthful Joseph Smith was left without further direct instructions from heaven regarding his mission. He continued to mature physically, emotionally, intellectually, and spiritually. Yet he was subject to what he called the "weakness of youth, and the foibles of human nature." He admitted to being "guilty of levity, and sometimes [of having] associated with jovial company, etc., not consistent with that character which ought to be maintained by one who was called of God as [he] had been." (JS-H 1:28.)

Feeling condemned for his "weakness and imperfections," Joseph sought for further guidance from God regarding his standing and his mission. On the evening of September 21, 1823, he approached the Lord in prayer with "full confidence" that he would receive an answer. In response, he was given a marvelous manifestation. An angel whose "whole person was glorious beyond description and [whose] countenance [was] truly like lightning" appeared and spent a good part of the night instructing Joseph. (JS-H 1:29–47.)

This messenger sent from the presence of God said his name was Moroni. He told the Prophet of a sacred record containing the "fulness of the everlasting Gospel" (v. 34) and an account of the ministry of the resurrected Savior to the ancient inhabitants of the western hemisphere. Moroni himself had been one of the prophets who had ministered to these ancient people, and he was the one who had buried the record for safekeeping prior to his death sometime after A.D. 421. The angel Moroni informed Joseph that in due time he was to be entrusted with this record and the means whereby he could translated it. The young man was strictly counseled that his whole purpose in obtaining the record, which was recorded on gold plates, should be to "glorify God" and to build His kingdom. (V. 46.)

The angel appeared to Joseph Smith on three occasions on that momentous night. In each instance, this messenger from God gave the young prophet the same instructions, adding some additional prophecies and cautions on the second and third visit. Obviously the message needed to be indelibly imprinted on the impressionable mind of the youthful prophet. Joseph was warned that Satan would try to tempt him to use the gold plates for his personal gain and not for God's purposes.

How quickly this warning would become reality. The following day, Joseph went to the location where the plates were buried, a place that was later to become known by millions worldwide as the Hill Cumorah. He knew the place the instant he arrived because he had seen it clearly in vision the night before. Removing the earth and a large stone that kept the plates hidden from mortal view, Joseph eagerly reached for the plates but was prevented from obtaining them by some unseen but very real power from God.

The heavenly messenger Moroni once more stood by the prophet's side and chastized him for worldly thoughts, which had evidently crossed his mind as he viewed the gold plates before him. There followed a vision wherein the budding prophet was shown the prince of darkness and an innumerable group of his evil followers. These wicked ones would fiercely oppose the coming forth of this additional testament of Jesus Christ.

The Prophet's mother, Lucy Mack Smith, reported that this vision of the forces of evil impressed her son "in such a striking manner, that the impression was always vivid in his memory until the very end of his days; and in giving a relation of this circumstance, not long prior to his death [in 1844], he remarked, that ever afterwards he was willing to keep the commandments of God." (*History of Joseph Smith by His Mother,* ed. Preston Nibley [Salt Lake City: Bookcraft, 1958], p. 81.)

Tutored by Heavenly Messengers

According to the Lord's timetable, the time was not right for Joseph to bring the plates forth from the earth and commence to translate them. He was instructed to return to that same place in one year, where the angel Moroni would meet him, and to continue that pattern until the time came for obtaining the plates. These annual visits continued for four years, from 1823 through 1827. Joseph said that each time he went to the Hill Cumorah he was met by Moroni "and received instruction and intelligence from him at each of our interviews, respecting what the Lord was going to do, and how and in what manner his kingdom was to be conducted in the last days." (JS-H 1:54.)

Apparently, a description of the civilization of the ancient inhabitants of the Americas was included in the instructions that Joseph Smith received. The Prophet's mother wrote that the family gathered frequently to be instructed by her young son. "During our evening conversations," she said, "Joseph would occasionally give us some of the most amusing recitals that could be imagined. He would describe the ancient inhabitants of this continent, their dress, mode of traveling, and the animals upon which they rode; their cities, their buildings, with every particular; their mode of warfare; and also their religious worship. This he would do with as much ease, seemingly, as if he had spent his whole life among them." (*History of Joseph Smith,* p. 83.)

The young Prophet was likely granted seeric glimpses of the people and circumstances, which he afterward described to his family. In addition to seeing seericly, Joseph was actually visited and instructed by some of these ancient inhabitants. As already mentioned, Joseph's annual tutor Moroni had been one of the prophets who had served among these people. Mormon, Nephi, "and others of the ancient Prophets who formerly lived on this Continent . . . came to him and communicated to him certain principles pertaining to the Gospel of the Son of God." (*Journal of Discourses,* 17:374; see also 15:185.) In a later recounting of his experiences, the Prophet Joseph Smith said that he "received many visits from the *angels* of God" prior to receiving the plates from "the *angel* of the Lord." (*History of the Church,* 4:537; italics added.)

Although Moroni is mentioned as having "the keys of the record of the stick of Ephraim" (D&C 27:5) — the plates from which the Book of Mormon was translated — we have no evidence that any of the angels or heavenly messengers who visited the young prophet during the years of 1823 to 1827 gave him any keys of priesthood authority. Elder George Q. Cannon said:

> If you will read the history of the Church from the beginning, you will find that Joseph was visited by various angelic beings, but not one of them professed to give him the keys until John the Baptist came to him. Moroni, who held the keys of the record of the stick of Ephraim, visited Joseph; he had doubtless, also, visits from Nephi and it may be from Alma and others, but though they came and had authority, holding the authority of the

Priesthood, we have no account of their ordaining him, neither did Joseph ever profess, because of the ministration of these angels, to have authority to administer in any of the ordinances of the Kingdom of God. (*Journal of Discourses,* 13:47.)

Keys of the Priesthood Restored

Though called as a prophet of God and given a specific work to do in translating the ancient record that Moroni had delivered into his hands, not until 1829 did Joseph Smith receive priesthood authority. Elder Cannon summarized Joseph's circumstances as follows: "When Joseph Smith desired baptism, though angels had visited him and had ministered unto him, though he had heard the voice of God and Jesus Christ, though he had been called to be a prophet, he had not the right and the authority to go forth and administer the ordinances of baptism, neither had any living soul, to do it legitimately. It was necessary that he should be ordained; it was necessary that those keys should be restored." (*Journal of Discourses,* 13:48.)

The restoration of priesthood keys authorizing baptism had been promised by Moroni on the night of September 22, 1823. On that occasion the heavenly messenger had declared, "When they [the gold plates] are interpreted [translated], the Lord will give the holy priesthood to some, and they shall begin to proclaim the gospel and baptize by water, and after that they shall have power to give the Holy Ghost by the laying on of their hands." (History, 1832, Joseph Smith Letterbook 1, Church Archives, p. 6.)

The keys of the priesthood would be restored in stages. First would come the restoration of the Aaronic Priesthood, authorizing baptism by water, and "after that" would come the restoration of the higher or Melchizedek Priesthood, authorizing the baptism of the Spirit—the laying on of hands for the gift of the Holy Ghost.

While translating the plates, Joseph Smith and his scribe Oliver Cowdery pondered passages in the text that spoke of baptism. Recognizing their need for this saving ordinance, they concluded to take the matter to the Lord in prayer. On May 15, 1829, while they were in the act of calling upon God, "a messenger from heaven descended in a cloud of light" and, laying his hands upon the two men, ordained them to the Aaronic Priesthood, conferring upon them the keys of this order of the priesthood. The messenger identified himself as the resurrected John the Baptist and said that this priesthood held the keys *"of the gospel of repentance, and of baptism by immersion for the remission of sins,"* but did not have "the power of laying on hands for the gift of the Holy Ghost." This power was promised to be given them at a later time. (JS-H 1:68–73; see also D&C 13:1; 27:7–8.)

Speaking of the significance of this sacred occasion, Elder George Q. Cannon said:

> John had the right to baptize when he was upon the earth; he held the keys of that Priesthood. He baptized Jesus by virtue of the Priesthood which he held; and those keys had not been taken from him. At the time when Joseph Smith was ordained, there was no man on the face of the earth that held the keys of the Priesthood and the authority to ordain him. If there had been a man in . . . any other church extant upon the face of the earth, who had the keys of the Priesthood, Joseph Smith would not have been ordained by an angel, because the keys would have been here and been bestowed by the man who held them. (*Journal of Discourses,* 13:47.)

Those priesthood keys, now restored, had long been absent from the earth. The death of John the Baptist at the hands of the wicked Herod had not brought baptism to an end. Jesus had given this authority to His apostles, who continued to authorize the administration of this saving ordinance in addition to other ordinances of the higher priesthood among the faithful who joined the Church of Jesus Christ. However, with the death of the early apostles, and after the removal of the Apostle John from among the people in general, the early Church fell into a state of apostasy, and none were authorized to continue in the authority of the priesthood.

The Higher Priesthood Restored

When John the Baptist appeared to Joseph Smith and Oliver Cowdery, he informed them that he was acting "under the direction of Peter, James and John, who held the keys of the Priesthood of Melchizedek, which Priesthood, he said, would in due time be conferred on [Joseph and Oliver]." (JS-H 1:72.) The two men did not have to wait long for the fulfillment of this promise.

Sometime between May 15 and May 29, 1829, Christ's three chief apostles appeared to Joseph and Oliver near the banks of the Susquehanna River (in which they had been baptized the previous month) and conferred upon them the higher or Melchizedek Priesthood. (See D&C 128:20; see also Larry C. Porter, "Dating the Restoration of the Melchizedek Priesthood," *Ensign,* June 1979, pp. 4–10.)

The Lord later spoke of this restoration of priesthood keys: "Peter, and James, and John . . . I have sent unto you, by whom I have ordained you and confirmed you to be apostles, and especial witnesses of my name, and bear the keys of your ministry and of the same things which I revealed unto them; unto whom I have committed the keys of my kingdom, and a dispensation of the gospel for the last times; and for the fulness of times, in the which I will gather together in one all things, both which are in heaven, and which are on earth." (D&C 27:12–13.)

Brigham Young noted the significance of Joseph Smith's

ordination by Christ's chief apostles: "Joseph Smith was a Prophet, Seer, and Revelator before he had power to build up the kingdom of God, or take the first step towards it. When did he obtain that power? Not until the angel[s] had ordained him to be an Apostle." (*Journal of Discourses,* 6:320; see also 18:239–40 and Orson Pratt, 12:252.)

Speaking of the nature of this higher priesthood that had been conferred upon him, the Prophet Joseph Smith said:

> There are two Priesthoods spoken of in the Scriptures, viz., the Melchizedek and the Aaronic or Levitical. Although there are two Priesthoods, yet the Melchizedek Priesthood comprehends the Aaronic or Levitical Priesthood, and is the grand head, and holds the highest authority which pertains to the priesthood, and the keys of the Kingdom of God in all ages of the world to the latest posterity on the earth; and is the channel through which all knowledge, doctrine, the plan of salvation and every important matter is revealed from heaven. (*Teachings of Joseph Smith,* pp. 166–67.)

The significance of this priesthood to mankind is further illustrated in these words from the Lord: "This greater priesthood administereth the gospel and holdeth the key of the mysteries of the kingdom, even the key of the knowledge of God. Therefore, in the ordinances thereof, the power of godliness is manifest." (D&C 84:19–20.)

Additional Keys Restored

Although the keys of the priesthood authorizing baptism and the laying on of hands had now been restored, other keys were yet to be granted in the gradual unfolding of the Lord's kingdom in the latter days. The Lord, in His wisdom, reveals "line upon line" those keys and doctrines that He wants mankind to possess. (See 2 Ne. 28:30; D&C 98:12; A of F 1:9.)

Almost one year later, on April 6, 1830, the Church was officially organized, with Joseph Smith being sustained as the "first elder" and Oliver Cowdery as the "second elder." (D&C 20:1–3.) As the Church grew over the next few years, various offices would be added to meet the needs of its expanding organization. Each office would grow out of the priesthood, with different administrative responsibilities, but not adding anything to the priesthood itself.

There were, however, additional keys of authority to be restored. Anciently, Peter had promised that before the second coming of Jesus Christ, there would be a "restitution of all things." (Acts 3:21.) In his day, the chief apostle of the Lord had been with the Savior and two of his fellow apostles on the Mount of Transfiguration when keys of authority were given. (See Matt. 17.) On that occasion, these three apostles received the keys of the kingdom from the prophets Moses and Elijah. (See Bruce R. McConkie, *Doctrinal New Testament Commentary,* 3 vols. [Salt Lake City: Bookcraft, 1965–73], 1:400; *Teachings of Joseph Smith,* p. 158.)

Those same keys needed to be restored to the earth in the latter days. On April 3, 1836, a modern-day Mount of Transfiguration experience occurred in the Kirtland Temple in Ohio. On that occasion, the two presiding elders of The Church of Jesus Christ of Latter-day Saints—Joseph Smith and Oliver Cowdery—were visited by the resurrected Redeemer and several other heavenly messengers. (See D&C 110.)

Moses appeared and, in a repeat of an act he had performed about eighteen hundred years earlier, he restored "the keys of the gathering of Israel from the four parts of the earth, and the leading of the ten tribes from the land of the north." (D&C 110:11.) Moses had originally received those keys on the slopes of Sinai, "when he was called and sent to lead Israel from Egypt to the promised land which the Lord had given to their father Abraham. He gathered Israel, and while he was not privileged to place them in possession of the [promised] land, nevertheless the keys were in his hands for the gathering. He came to Peter, James, and John on the mount at the transfiguration and there bestowed upon them the same keys for the gathering of Israel in the days in which they lived." (Joseph Fielding Smith, *Doctrines of Salvation,* 3 vols., comp. Bruce R. McConkie [Salt Lake City: Bookcraft, 1954–56], 3:257.)

The next heavenly messenger to appear in the Kirtland Temple was *Elias.* Elder James E. Talmage explained that the name Elias means a "forerunner, or one sent of God to prepare the way for greater developments in the gospel plan." (*Jesus the Christ,* 25th ed. [Salt Lake City: Deseret Book, 1956], p. 375.)

While the title of Elias has been applied to a number of ancient prophets, *the* Elias who appeared on this occasion has been identified by President Joseph Fielding Smith as the Angel Gabriel, or Noah. (See *Answers to Gospel Questions,* 5 vols., comp. Joseph Fielding Smith, Jr. [Salt Lake City: Deseret Book, 1957–66], 3:138–41.) He committed to Joseph and Oliver the keys of "the dispensation of the gospel of Abraham," stating that in them and their posterity "all generations after [them] should be blessed." (D&C 110:12.) The Lord referred to the keys Elias possessed as "the keys of bringing to pass the restoration of all things spoken by the mouth of all the holy prophets since the world began." (D&C 27:6.)

Elder Bruce R. McConkie said:

> Now what was the *gospel of Abraham* [restored by Elias]? Obviously it was the commission, the mission, the endowment and power, the message of salvation, given to Abraham. . . . It was a divine promise that both in the world and out of the world his seed should con-

tinue "as innumerable as the stars; or, if ye were to count the sand upon the seashore ye could not number them. . . . "

Thus the gospel of Abraham was one of celestial marriage; . . . it was a gospel commission to provide a lineage for the elect portion of the [premortal] spirits. . . . This power and commission is what Elias restored. (*Mormon Doctrine,* 2d ed. [Salt Lake City: Bookcraft, 1966], pp. 219–20; see also Hoyt W. Brewster, Jr., *Doctrine and Covenants Encyclopedia* [Salt Lake City: Bookcraft, 1988] p. 139.)

The final heavenly messenger to appear on that sacred occasion was the prophet Elijah. (See D&C 110:13–16.) He came in fulfillment of the prophecy of the Old Testament prophet Malachi who promised that Elijah would come to "turn the heart of the fathers to the children, and the heart of the children to their fathers." (Mal. 4:5–6; see also 3 Ne. 25:5–6; D&C 2:1; JS-H 1:38–39.) Joseph Smith stated that the word *turn* should actually be rendered as *seal.* (*Teachings of Joseph Smith,* p. 323.)

To turn or seal one's heart to the fathers is to seek after the records of one's ancestors, and then to vicariously perform the saving ordinances of the gospel of Jesus Christ in their behalf. In this saving work, this work of redemption, families are linked together in covenant sealings that bind them together eternally.

The priesthood keys that Elijah restored were the sealing powers that validate all priesthood ordinances. "That sealing power puts the stamp of approval upon *every ordinance* that is done in this Church and *more particularly those that are performed in the temples of the Lord,*" declared President Joseph Fielding Smith. (*Doctrines of Salvation,* 3:129.) This priesthood authority and power allows the ordinances to be "administered in righteousness." (*Teachings of Joseph Smith,* p. 172.)

Acting under the direction of Jesus Christ, the prophet Elijah had given the same keys, the sealing power of the priesthood, to the Savior's three chief apostles on the Mount of Transfiguration in an earlier dispensation. (See Smith, *Doctrines of Salvation,* 2:107–12.) (The account we presently have in the King James Bible uses the name of "Elias," which is the Aramaic version of the Hebrew "Elijah.") There may well have been other heavenly messengers present on that occasion, including John the Baptist, who was an "Elias," but no other messenger held the keys that were to be delivered by the prophet Elijah. (See McConkie, *Commentary,* 1:400–403.)

Other heavenly messengers appeared to the Prophet Joseph Smith during his period of preparation and presidency. For example, we know that an angel named Raphael visited the Prophet. (See D&C 128:21.) Michael, or Adam, intervened in Joseph's behalf when the devil sought to deceive the Prophet on one sacred occasion. (See D&C 128:20; see also Brewster, *Encyclopedia,* pp. 16–17.) In addition, "divers angels, from Michael or Adam down to the present time" visited Joseph Smith, "giving line upon line, precept upon precept." (D&C 128:21.)

Thus, line upon line, the Lord instructed the Prophet Joseph Smith and conferred upon him the keys of the kingdom of God on earth. While Joseph was the "first elder" of the Church, he shared these keys for a time with the "second elder," Oliver Cowdery. These two men initially stood as joint witnesses at the head of the dispensation of the fullness of times when the gospel with all its saving ordinances, covenants, and principles was restored to the earth to prepare mankind for the second coming of the Lord Jesus Christ.

Chapter 3

The Order of Succession in Joseph Smith's Day

The Prophet and the President

Joseph Smith was called of God to be His prophet. (See D&C 1:17; 3:9; 18:8.) No mortal man gave Joseph this calling. His appointment as God's prophet, holding the keys of the kingdom, stood independent of his later calling to preside over the Church. Brigham Young gave the following explanation:

> Does a man's being a *Prophet* in this Church prove that he shall be the *President* of it? I answer, no! A man may be a Prophet, Seer, and Revelator, and it may have nothing to do with his being the President of the Church. Suffice it to say, that Joseph was the President of the Church, as long as he lived: the people chose to have it so. He always filled that responsible station, by the voice of the people. Can you find any revelation *appointing* him the *President* of the Church? The *keys* of the *Priesthood* were committed to Joseph, to build up the *Kingdom of God* on the *earth,* and were not to be taken from him

in time or in eternity; but when he was called to preside over the Church, it was by the voice of the people, though he held the keys of the *Priesthood, Independent* of their voice. (*Journal of Discourses,* 1:133; italics added.)

This distinction is made whenever the members of the Church sustain the General Authorities. For example, at the April 1991 general conference, the members sustained "Ezra Taft Benson as prophet, seer, and revelator and President" of the Church, then shortly after, they sustained "the Counselors [in the First Presidency] and the Twelve Apostles as prophets, seers, and revelators." ("The Sustaining of Church Officers," *Ensign,* May 1991, p. 6.) Though the office of prophet and President stand independent of one another, since the days of Joseph Smith, each man called to be President and sustained by the members of The Church of Jesus Christ of Latter-day Saints has also been a prophet. It is inconceivable that the Saints would reject as the administrative leader of the Church the man who holds the keys of priesthood authority.

Oliver Cowdery as Second Elder

Oliver Cowdery entered the Prophet Joseph Smith's life on April 5, 1829. He had been prompted by the Spirit to visit the Prophet and to inquire about the Book of Mormon, which he had heard so much about. Two days later, Oliver commenced work as Joseph's scribe, a time he would later refer to as "days never to be forgotten — to sit under the sound of a voice dictated by the inspiration of heaven." (JS-H 1:71, note.)

Oliver's work with Joseph Smith on the Book of Mormon led to an outpouring of marvelous spiritual experiences. He was the recipient of a number of revelations found in the Doctrine and Covenants, and his name is second only to Joseph Smith in being mentioned the most times in that compilation of revelatory writ. The Lord chose him to serve as one of the Three Witnesses to the Book of Mormon, and along with the other witnesses, he was given the charge to seek out the twelve men to be called to the first apostolic quorum of this dispensation. (See D&C 18:9, 26–37.)

Oliver was present when the keys of the Aaronic and Melchizedek Priesthoods were restored and was a corecipient of those keys with the Prophet Joseph Smith. (See D&C 13:1; 27:8, 12–13; 128:20.) When the Church of Jesus Christ was restored to earth in this dispensation on April 6, 1830, Joseph and Oliver were sustained as the teachers and spiritual advisers of the members of the Church.

Oliver was the "second elder" of the Church. (D&C 20: 1–3.) Thus, in the beginning, he stood by Joseph Smith's side as his successor, holding the same keys that the Prophet held, but he was subservient to the "first elder" of the Church. (See, for example, D&C 20:1–5. Note that the terms "first elder" and "second elder" were added to the original revelation in 1835 when it was published as part of the Doctrine and Covenants. Prior to this time the wording was simply "elder." However, from the onset Oliver's position was clearly secondary to Joseph's.)

Joseph Smith Held the Keys

On several occasions the Lord revealed that Joseph Smith held the keys of the kingdom and that no other man or woman had this authority. For example, in September of 1830, the Lord reminded Oliver Cowdery that "no one shall be appointed to receive commandments and revelations in this church excepting my servant Joseph Smith, Jun., for he receiveth them even as Moses." (D&C 28:2.)

This revelation came as a result of Oliver's having been wrongly influenced by a man claiming to receive revelation regarding the building of Zion. The Lord not only reminded

Oliver of Joseph's singular right to receive revelation for the Church, but He also reprimanded him. Oliver was told not to "command him who is at thy head, and at the head of the church." (D&C 28:6.)

In this same revelation the Lord said that Joseph would retain the keys until the Lord appointed another to take his place. (See v. 7.) This statement was essentially repeated in a revelation given in December of 1830. The Lord said Joseph would retain the keys if he remained faithful "and if not, another will I plant in his stead." (D&C 35:18.)

In February of 1831, the Lord made a slight modification in the procedures governing succession. While Jesus Christ would always select the man to lead His church on earth and serve as His prophet, He gave to Joseph Smith some significant authority in the matter. The Savior declared that, if the power be taken from Joseph Smith (ostensibly through transgression), "he [Joseph] shall not have power except to appoint another in his stead." (D&C 43:4.)

While at first thought this may seem strange — giving a fallen prophet the power to appoint (ordain) his successor — it really was a safeguard against false prophets. Under these guidelines, if a man claimed that Joseph Smith was a fallen prophet and that the Lord had selected him to take the Prophet's place, one would merely have to ask the claimant if he had been ordained to this calling by Joseph Smith. If he had not, then the claim could be quickly dismissed. Because the Lord knows the end from the beginning, this procedure was not likely ever intended to be used. But it did provide a stopgap to any pretenders to authority.

By September of 1831 there were some who sought to discredit or to criticize the Prophet "without cause." (D&C 64:6.) In response to this, the Lord declared: "The keys of the mysteries of the kingdom shall not be taken from my servant Joseph Smith, Jun., through the means I have appointed, while he liveth, inasmuch as he obeyeth mine ordinances." (D&C 64:5.)

Almost two years after this revelation, Joseph received the assurance that he would not fall and that "the keys of this kingdom shall never be taken from you, while thou art in the world, neither in the world to come." (D&C 90:3.) Commenting on this latest revelation, President Joseph Fielding Smith wrote:

> Here we have the assurance that the Prophet would endure to the end, and that he had proved himself worthy to stand at the head of the Dispensation of the Fulness of Times. The keys are now committed into his hands, and he will stand at the head of this dispensation in the grand council when it shall be held, and they will be in his possession eternally. At the head of this dispensation he will preside under Adam who holds the keys of all dispensations pertaining to this earth, and Adam holds them under the direction of Jesus Christ, the Holy One of Israel, who has all power and authority under His Father. (*Church History and Modern Revelation,* 2 vols. [Salt Lake City: The Council of the Twelve Apostles, 1953], 1:388.)

Joseph Smith's standing as God's prophet was assured. He would preside as the living prophet while on earth, and after he passed through the veil of death, he would continue to preside as the prophet of this last dispensation. However, the keys to conduct the affairs of the kingdom of God on earth would remain; for prior to his death, Joseph would confer these keys upon another mortal prophet who would preside over the Church on earth.

The Presidency of the High Priesthood

Although a revelation given in November of 1831 had mentioned "the First Presidency of the Melchizedek Priesthood" (D&C 68:15), it was not until January 25, 1832, that Joseph Smith was sustained as the President of the High (Melchizedek) Priesthood in a conference of the Church (see Brewster, *Encyclopedia*, p. 437). In a later revelation regarding this office, the Lord declared: "Wherefore, it must needs be that one be appointed of the High Priesthood to preside over the priesthood, and he shall be called President of the High Priesthood of the Church. Or, in other words, the Presiding High Priest over the High Priesthood of the Church." (D&C 107:65–66.)

On March 8, 1832, the Prophet selected Jesse Gause and Sidney Rigdon to serve as his counselors in the presidency of the High Priesthood. In an unpublished revelation given that same month, the Lord said: "Unto the office of the presidency of the high priesthood I have given authority to preside with assistance of his councilors over all concerns of the church." (Kirtland Revelation Book, Joseph Smith Collection, Historical Department, The Church of Jesus Christ of Latter-day Saints, pp. 10–11.) In a revelation given in March of 1832, the Lord declared that "the keys of the kingdom . . . belong always unto the Presidency of the High Priesthood." (D&C 81:2.)

Jesse Gause, however, "failed to continue in a manner consistent with this appointment, [and] the call was subsequently transferred to Frederick G. Williams." (D&C 81: heading; see also Brewster, *Encyclopedia*, pp. 203–4.) On March 8, 1833, the Lord said to the Prophet Joseph Smith: "Verily I say unto thy brethren, Sidney Rigdon and Frederick G. Williams, their sins are forgiven them also, and they are accounted as equal with thee in holding the keys of this last kingdom." (D&C 90:6.)

Joseph Smith, Sidney Rigdon, and Frederick G. Williams—the three presiding high priests—formed "a quorum of the Presidency of the Church." (D&C 107:22.) This presidency was "to preside in council, and set in order all the affairs of this church and kingdom." (D&C 90:16.) While the President obviously presided over all affairs, the counselors in the presidency had authority to act in behalf of the President in his absence or as assigned by him.

David Whitmer Is Designated as Joseph's Successor

Among the most prominent participants of the early period in Church history was David Whitmer. He was one of the six original members of the Church, as well as one of the three privileged to see the angel Moroni, behold the gold plates from which the Book of Mormon was translated (among other ancient artifacts), and hear the voice of God bearing personal testimony to the truthfulness of the ancient record of holy writ.

David surfaced in the order of succession in July of 1834. In the spring of that year, a body of some two hundred Latter-day Saints known as Zion's Camp commenced a thousand-mile journey from Ohio to Missouri. The purpose of this expedition was to "redeem" Zion, or to assist the persecuted Saints in Missouri in obtaining redress for all the wrongs they had suffered. (See D&C 101:55–60; 103:29–40.)

Upon arriving in Missouri, the Prophet Joseph, who was commander-in-chief of the expedition, was informed by the Lord that in consequence of transgression, the time for Zion's redemption was not yet at hand. (See D&C 105.) A conference was called the first week of July in Missouri, and during the course of its proceedings, the following took place:

> While the conference was in session, Joseph Smith presiding, he arose and said that the time had come when he must appoint his successor in office. Some have supposed that it would be Oliver Cowdery; but, said he, Oliver has lost that privilege in consequence of transgression. The Lord has made it known to me that

David Whitmer is the man. David was then called forward, and Joseph and his counsellors laid hands upon him, and ordained him to his station, to succeed him. Joseph then gave David a charge, in the hearing of the whole assembly. Joseph then seemed to rejoice that that work was done, and said, now brethren, if anything should befall me, the work of God will roll on with more power than it has hitherto done. Then brethren, you will have a man who can lead you as well as I can. He will be Prophet, Seer, Revelator, and Translator before God. (*Ensign of Liberty* 1, no. 3 [December 1847]: 43–44; see also *History of the Church,* 3:32.)

Evidently Joseph had not discussed this with his newly designated successor, for David was later to say, "I did not know what he was going to do until he laid his hands upon me and ordained me." (*An Address to All Believers in Christ* [Richmond, Virginia: David Whitmer, 1887], p. 55.)

In addition to being designated as Joseph Smith's successor, David also became the "President of Zion" (presiding officer of that stake of the Church in Missouri) and was given John Whitmer and W. W. Phelps as his counselors. The Prophet also organized a high council to serve with this newly called presidency.

Unfortunately, though David remained faithful in his testimony of the Book of Mormon, he did not remain faithful to the Church. As a result, on February 4, 1838, a general assembly of the Saints in Far West, Missouri, withdrew the hand of fellowship from him and rejected him as their presiding officer. The high council at Far West excommunicated him on April 13, 1838, which action was upheld by the Prophet. (See *History of the Church,* 3:32, note.) Among the charges levied against David Whitmer was that he wrongly claimed to be the "President of the Church of Christ" in Missouri. (*History of the Church,* 3:18–19.) Apparently David mistakenly considered his position as a local stake president in Missouri on a par with Joseph Smith's presiding position. This may have been the result of the First Presidency's acting as the stake presidency in Kirtland, Ohio, in addition to their presiding over the entire Church.

David claimed that the council had no jurisdiction over him. He did not understand that his calling as *a* president over the Church in Missouri was not equal with Joseph Smith's presiding authority over the entire Church. Furthermore, at the time of his excommunication, David appeared not to have understood the changed nature of his appointment as Joseph Smith's designated successor as a result of an appointment that came to Oliver Cowdery in December of 1834.

Assistant President of the Church

As previously noted, Oliver Cowdery's standing as the *second* elder of the Church initially placed him next to the Prophet Joseph as the presiding officer of the Church. He stood by Joseph's side every time keys of priesthood authority were restored to the earth by heavenly messengers sent from the presence of God.

On the evening of December 5, 1834, Joseph was in a meeting with his two counselors in the presidency as well as Oliver Cowdery, "conversing upon the welfare of the Church." During the course of that meeting, the Prophet laid his hands upon Oliver's head and "ordained him an assistant-president, saying these words: 'In the name of Jesus Christ, who was crucified for the sins of the world, I lay my hands upon thee and ordain thee an assistant-president to the High and Holy Priesthood, in the Church of the Latter-day Saints.' " (*History of the Church,* 2:176.)

Oliver explained that this ordination took place in fulfillment of the promise "made by the Angel [John the Baptist] while in company with President Smith, at the time they received the office of the lesser priesthood." (Historian's Book A1, Historical Department, The Church of Jesus Christ of Latter-day Saints, p. 17. He learned that "the office of Assistant President is to assist in presiding over the whole Church, and to officiate in the absence of the President." (Manuscript History of the Church, Book A-1, Historical Department, The Church of Jesus Christ of Latter-day Saints, 5 Dec. 1834; see also Smith, *Doctrines of Salvation*, 1:211–213.)

There was no question in the minds of Joseph's counselors that Oliver took precedence over each of them. His signature preceded those of the counselors on official Church documents. Furthermore, in the 1835 edition of the Doctrine and Covenants, Oliver was officially designated as the "second elder" in the Church, although prior to this time he had already been recognized as second to Joseph Smith and named as an apostle and an elder in the Church.

Others had been designated as assistant presidents of the Church, acting essentially in the role of a counselor, but none held the priesthood keys bestowed upon Oliver Cowdery. In this sense, his office was more as an Associate President. (See Robert Glen Mouritsen, "The Office of Associate President of The Church of Jesus Christ of Latter-day Saints," Master's thesis, Brigham Young University, 1972.)

President Joseph Fielding Smith said the following regarding Oliver Cowdery's importance in the hierarchy of the Church: "Oliver Cowdery was called to be what? The 'Second Elder' of the Church, the 'Second President' of the Church. We leave him out in our list of Presidents of the Church . . . *but he was an Assistant President. Oliver Cowdery's standing in the beginning was as the 'Second Elder' of the Church, holding the keys jointly with the Prophet Joseph Smith.*" (*Doctrines of Salvation*, 1:212.)

38

The Apostolic Office

A development that took place shortly after Oliver Cowdery's ordination as the Associate President of the Church was the establishment of the Quorum of the Twelve Apostles. Although a revelation given in June of 1829 had charged Oliver Cowdery and David Whitmer—two of the Three Witnesses to the Book of Mormon—to "search out the Twelve" (D&C 18:37), the apostles were not selected until February of 1835.

The Lord had designated Joseph Smith and Oliver Cowdery as apostles (see D&C 20:2–3), and David Whitmer and Martin Harris also appeared to have received that special calling. The Lord told Oliver and David that they were called "with that same calling with which [the Apostle Paul] was called." (D&C 18:9.) Brigham Young declared that "Joseph Smith, Oliver Cowdery, and David Whitmer were the first Apostles of this dispensation." (*Journal of Discourses,* 6:320.) And Heber C. Kimball noted: "Peter comes along with James and John and ordains Joseph to be an Apostle, and then Joseph ordains Oliver, and David Whitmer, and Martin Harris; and then they were ordered to select twelve more and ordain them." (*Journal of Discourses,* 6:29.)

One of the Three Witnesses to the Book of Mormon, Martin Harris, was not mentioned in the 1829 revelation as one charged with searching out the Twelve. At that particular time, he was "out of favor with the Lord" and for that reason his name might have been omitted from the revelation. However, it appears that all three of the men known as the Three Witnesses were to receive the responsibility of selecting the Twelve who were to be special witnesses to the Lord Jesus Christ. (*History of the Church,* 2:186–87, note.)

On February 8, 1835, Joseph Smith related to Brigham and Joseph Young a vision he had received. During the course of their conversation, the Prophet informed Brigham Young that he was to become one of the "twelve Special Witnesses" who were to be called "to open the door of the Gospel to foreign nations." (*History of the Church*, 2:181, note.) Six days later, a general meeting was convened in Kirtland, where, following prayer and a blessing by the presidency of the Church, the Three Witnesses selected the twelve men to serve in the first Quorum of the Twelve Apostles in this dispensation.

The twelve men selected were Lyman E. Johnson, Brigham Young, Heber C. Kimball, Orson Hyde, David W. Patten, Luke S. Johnson, William E. M'Lellin, John F. Boynton, Orson Pratt, William Smith, Thomas B. Marsh, and Parley P. Pratt. The first three of these men — Lyman E. Johnson, Brigham Young, and Heber C. Kimball — were called forward and ordained under the hands of the Three Witnesses, with the blessing being confirmed by the First Presidency. (See *History of the Church*, 2:187–188, note.)

The following day, February 15, six more were ordained: Orson Hyde, David W. Patten, Luke S. Johnson, William E. M'Lellin, John F. Boynton, and William Smith. It is of interest to note that in a letter Oliver Cowdery later sent to Brigham Young, Oliver indicated that Phineas Young had initially been selected as one of the Twelve rather than William Smith. However, Joseph Smith allegedly prevailed upon the Three Witnesses to select his brother William in the place of Phineas. (See Journal History, Historical Department, The Church of Jesus Christ of Latter-day Saints, February 27, 1848.) Parley P. Pratt was ordained to the apostleship on February 21, Thomas B. Marsh on April 25, and Orson Pratt on April 26, 1835. (See Joseph Fielding Smith, *Essentials in Church History* [Salt Lake City: Deseret Book, 1979], p. 152.)

The Prophet Joseph later arranged the order of seniority among the Twelve according to their ages, with the eldest being senior and the youngest being junior. This resulted in

Lyman E. Johnson's going from the first position to the last. The following chart illustrates the order of seniority of the apostles according to three criteria:

Name of Apostle	Order Called	Order Ordained	Order of Seniority
Lyman E. Johnson	1	1	12
Brigham Young	2	2	3
Heber C. Kimball	3	3	4
Orson Hyde	4	4	5
David W. Patten	5	5	2
Luke S. Johnson	6	6	8
William E. M'Lellin	7	7	6
John F. Boynton	8	8	11
Orson Pratt	9	12	10
William Smith	10	9	9
Thomas B. Marsh	11	11	1
Parley P. Pratt	12	10	7

Within three years from the time of their ordination, four of these men lost their apostleship through apostasy and excommunication: John F. Boynton, Luke S. Johnson, Lyman E. Johnson, and William E. M'Lellin. By October of 1838, Thomas B. Marsh had apostatized, and David W. Patten was martyred. Thus, by any measurement of seniority, Brigham Young ascended to the senior position among the Twelve Apostles.

The Initial Limitations on the Ministry of the Twelve

Initially the ministry of the Twelve Apostles was limited, and their full authority to stand next to the First Presidency came "line upon line." On February 27, 1835, the Prophet Joseph Smith gave the following instructions regarding the duties of the Twelve:

They are the Twelve Apostles, who are called to the office of the Traveling High Council, who are to preside over the churches of the Saints, among the Gentiles, where there is *no* presidency established; and they are to travel and preach among the Gentiles until the Lord shall command them to go to the Jews. They are to hold the keys of this ministry, to unlock the door of the Kingdom of heaven unto all nations, and to preach the Gospel to every creature. This is the power, authority, and virtue of their apostleship. (Kirtland Council Minute Book, p. 88, manuscript, Church Archives; italics added.)

At the time the Twelve Apostles were organized, they were a "traveling high council" that did not have authority to preside in areas where a stake presidency and a "standing high council" existed. Two stakes were then extant, one in Kirtland and one in Missouri. On May 2, 1835, the Prophet Joseph said the following regarding this limitation: "The Twelve will have no right to go into Zion, or any of its stakes, and there undertake to regulate the affairs thereof, where there is a standing high council; but it is their duty to go abroad and regulate all matters relative to the different branches of the Church." (*History of the Church,* 2:220; see also Minutes of a Grand Council at Kirtland, Ohio, 2 May 1835, manuscript, included in Patriarchal Blessing Book 2, Church Archives.)

The Role of the Standing High Council

The Prophet Joseph Smith also placed limitations on the role of the "standing high council": "No standing High Council has authority to go into the churches abroad, and regulate the matters thereof, for this belongs to the Twelve." (*History of the Church,* 2:220.) The 1835 revelation designating the presiding quorums of the Church that were to be "equal in authority" also identified the "standing high councils, at the stakes of Zion" as forming "a quorum equal in authority in the affairs of the church, in all their decisions, to the quorum of the presidency, or to the traveling high council." (D&C 107:36–37.)

There is reason to believe that in these formative years of Church government, the standing high councils were an important part of the succession issue. In July of 1834, the Prophet organized a high council in Clay County, Missouri, under the presidency of David Whitmer, W. W. Phelps, and John Whitmer. Four of those called to serve on that council (William E. M'Lellin, Thomas B. Marsh, Orson Pratt, and Parley P. Pratt) were called the following year into the original group of men who comprised the Quorum of the Twelve Apostles.

Joseph Smith made the following observations regarding the organization of this high council:

> I gave the Council such instructions in relation to their high calling, as would enable them to proceed to minister in their office agreeable to the pattern heretofore given; read the revelation on the subject; and told them that *If I should now be taken away,* I had accomplished the great work the Lord had laid before me, and that which I had desired of the Lord; and that *I had done my duty in organizing the High Council, through which council the will of the Lord might be known on all important occasions, in the building up of Zion,* and establishing truth in the earth. (*History of the Church,* 2:124; italics added.)

Thus, in the developing days of Church government, the standing high councils stood in the line of succession. They were initially made "equal in authority" (D&C 107:36–37) to the Quorum of the Twelve (the traveling high council) and the Quorum of the Seventy at a time when the apostles had limited jurisdiction in the Church.

Emma Smith would later cite this revelation in contending that William Marks, the president of the Nauvoo Stake (and high council), should have succeeded her husband as the presiding officer of the Church. (See Journal of James M. Monroe, 24 April 1845, Yale University; cited in D. Michael Quinn, "The Mormon Succession Crisis of 1844," *Brigham Young University Studies* 16 (Winter 1976): 187–233, p. 214.) Marks himself did not pursue the presidency of the Church based on this revelation. He did, however, become an active participant in several schismatic groups that formed following the death of Joseph Smith.

Note that there has not been unanimity of feeling regarding the administrative authority of the standing high council. The historian Elder B. H. Roberts believed that such a council was limited in jurisdiction:

> The high council is a judicial and not a presiding or executive council, as is proven by the following:
>
> "The high council was appointed by revelation for the purpose of settling important difficulties which might arise in the church, which could not be settled by the church or the bishop's council to the satisfaction of the parties" (D&C 102:2).
>
> Hence the "equality" here referred to [D&C 107:36–37] must have reference to judicial not to administrative affairs in the Church. . . . The standing high council in a stake of Zion is a local council, limited in its operations to the particular district of [or] country comprising the stake. (*Succession in the Presidency of the Church of Jesus Christ of Latter-day Saints,* 2nd ed. [Salt Lake City: George Q. Cannon & Sons Publishing Co., 1900], p. 92.)

The Quorum of the Twelve Is Given an Expanded Ministry

Circumstances changed following the 1835 revelation, and "line upon line," the Quorum of the Twelve was given more authority and responsibility. Through their dedication to their ministry, the Twelve Apostles grew in stature and importance to the Church. Their highly successful missionary efforts in England were particularly impressive.

On August 16, 1841, the Prophet announced "that the time had come when the Twelve should be called upon to *stand in their place next to the First Presidency,* and attend to the settling of emigrants and the business of the Church *at the stakes,* and assist to bear off the kingdom victoriously to the nations." (*History of the Church,* 4:403; italics added.) Thus a significant step in the developing stature and authority of the Quorum of the Twelve was taken.

Not only did the Twelve assume more responsibility ecclesiastically, but they also became more involved in business and civic affairs. The apostles were called to assist the Prophet in handling the finances of the Church. Eleven of these men each served for a time on the Nauvoo City Council during the years of 1841–44. On January 28, 1842, Joseph received a revelation calling the Twelve to "take in hand the editorial department of the *Times and Seasons* [the official Church publication], according to that manifestation which shall be given unto them by the power of [the] Holy Spirit." (*History of the Church,* 4:503.)

The Twelve had begun to function in a significant measure next to the First Presidency. However, there were still keys of authority that had not been bestowed upon them and would not until just shortly before the Prophet's death.

Hyrum Smith Called as Associate President

One more important development in the presiding councils of the Church took place in January of 1841 that impacted the issue of succession. As previously mentioned, Oliver Cowdery had been the assistant or associate president of the Church, standing next to the Prophet Joseph in holding the keys of the kingdom of God on earth. Unfortunately, Oliver lost his keys and calling through apostasy and was excommunicated on April 11, 1838. Almost three years later Hyrum Smith was called by revelation to succeed Oliver as the second elder of the Church.

At the time of his call as the associate president, Hyrum was serving as second counselor in the First Presidency. The Lord revealed that Hyrum should be released from this calling and "take the office of Priesthood and Patriarch, which was appointed unto him by his father, by blessing and also by right." (D&C 124:91.) Hyrum's father, Joseph Smith, Sr., had been the Patriarch to the Church from 1833 until his death in 1840. The son was now to assume the patriarchal mantle of the father.

In addition to calling him as the Patriarch to the Church, the Lord also called Hyrum to "act in concert" with his prophet-brother, Joseph, "who shall show unto him the keys whereby he may ask and receive, and be crowned with the same blessing, and glory, and honor, and priesthood, and gifts of the priesthood, that once were put upon him that was my servant Oliver Cowdery." (D&C 124:95.) Thus, Hyrum Smith was called to hold the keys jointly with Joseph Smith, which placed him second only to the Prophet in the succession order of the Church.

President Joseph Fielding Smith made the following observation regarding Hyrum's station in the Church: "With many members of the Church Hyrum Smith was just the Patriarch. Hyrum Smith received a double portion. He received the office of Patriarch which belonged to his father and came to him by right, and also received the keys to be 'Second President' and precede the counselors [in the First Presidency] as Oliver Cowdery had done. So he would have *remained* as President of the Church had he not died a martyr." (*Doctrines of Salvation*, 1:221; italics added.)

Until his death at the hands of assassins in Carthage,

Illinois, on June 27, 1844, Hyrum stood next to the Prophet as *a* president of the Church, although it was understood that he was always second to Joseph. The Twelve recognized this position. Following the martyrdoms of Joseph and Hyrum Smith, Brigham Young declared: "If Hyrum had lived he would not have stood between Joseph and the Twelve but he would have stood for Joseph. — Did Joseph ordain any man to take his place? He did. Who was it? It was Hyrum, but, Hyrum fell a martyr before Joseph did." (*Times and Seasons* 5:683.)

The Twelve Receive the Fullness of the Keys of the Kingdom

Although designated by revelation (D&C 107:23–24; 112:30–32) and by the Prophet Joseph as the presiding body that stood next to the Presidency of the Church, the Twelve Apostles did not receive all of the keys of the kingdom until shortly before the martyrdoms of Joseph and Hyrum Smith. The Lord, who knows all things, and who thus knew of the impending deaths of His noble servants, inspired the Prophet Joseph Smith to confer every key of authority that he and Hyrum held upon the Twelve Apostles in the winter of 1843–44. A sampling of testimonies regarding this significant action follows.

> *Testimony of Wilford Woodruff:* Joseph Smith "organized the quorum of the Twelve, a few months before his death, to prepare them for the endowment[.] And when they received their endowment, and actually received the keys of the kingdom of God, . . . [Joseph] exclaimed, 'upon your shoulders the kingdom rests, and you must round up your shoulders, and bear it; for I have had to do it until now. But now the responsibility rests upon you. It mattereth not what becomes of me.' " (*Times and Seasons* 5:698.)

Testimony of Brigham Young: "Joseph told the Twelve, the year before he died, 'there is not one key or power to be bestowed on this church to lead the people into the celestial gate but I have given you, showed you, and talked it over to you; the kingdom is set up, and you have the perfect pattern, and you can go and build up the kingdom, and go in at the celestial gate, taking your train with you.' " (*Millennial Star* 10:115.)

Testimony of Parley P. Pratt: "This great and good man [Joseph Smith] was led, before his death, to call the Twelve together, from time to time, and to instruct them in all things pertaining to the kingdom, ordinances, and government of God. He often observed that he was laying the foundation, but it would remain for the Twelve to complete the building. Said he: 'I know not why; but for some reason I am constrained to hasten my preparations, and to confer upon the Twelve all the ordinances, keys, covenants, endowments, and sealing ordinances of the priesthood, and so set before them a pattern in all things pertaining to the sanctuary and the endowment therein.'

"Having done this, he rejoiced exceedingly; for, said he, the Lord is about to lay the burden on your shoulders and let me rest awhile; and if they kill me, continued he, the kingdom of God will roll on, as I have now finished the work which was laid upon me, by committing to you all things for the building up of the kingdom according to the heavenly vision, and the pattern shown me from heaven." (*Millennial Star* 5:151.)

Testimony of Orson Hyde: "Brother Joseph said some time before he was murdered, 'If I am taken away, upon you, the Twelve, will rest the responsibility of leading this people, and do not be bluffed off by any man. Go forward in the path of your duty though you walk into death. If you will be bold and maintain your ground the great God will sustain you.' " (*Times and Seasons* 5:650.)

Testimony of Heber C. Kimball: "Joseph has passed behind the vail and he pulled off his shoes, and some one else puts them on, until he passes the vail to Bro. Joseph. President [Brigham] Young is our president, and our head, and he puts the shoes on first. If Brother Hyrum had remained here, he would have put them on. Hyrum is gone with Joseph and is still his counsellor. The Twelve have received the keys of the kingdom and as long as there is one of them left, he will hold them in preference to any one else." (*Times and Seasons* 5:664.)

Thus, by the time the blood of two of the noblest men on earth was shed on that tragic afternoon of June 27, 1844, the Lord had already set in place the proper order of succession in His church. With the deaths of President Joseph Smith and his associate in the presidency, Hyrum Smith, the Twelve Apostles with Brigham Young at their head became the rightful ones to lead the Church and kingdom of God on earth.

Chapter 4

False Claims to Succession after the Prophet's Martyrdom

Sidney Rigdon

Sidney Rigdon was a formidable figure in the early days of the Church. He was a powerful preacher, and, like Aaron was for Moses (see Ex. 4:14–16), Sidney was called by revelation to be a spokesman for Joseph Smith (see D&C 100:9).

As mentioned in the previous chapter, Sidney Rigdon was called as a counselor in the presidency of the High Priesthood in 1832 and served as a first counselor in the First Presidency from 1833 until the death of the Prophet in 1844. However, during this period his faith seemed to ebb and flow according to the circumstances in which he found himself. On one occasion the Prophet Joseph said of his counselor: "Brother Sidney is a man whom I love, but he is not capable of that pure and steadfast love for those who are his benefactors that should characterize a President of the Church of Christ." (*History of the Church,* 1:443.)

"He was a man of admitted ability as an orator, but lacked discretion," noted B. H. Roberts. Sidney was

> a man of fervid imagination, but of inferior judgment; ambitious of place and honor, but without that steadiness of purpose and other qualities of soul which in time secure them. In the early years of The Church he suffered much for the cause of God, but he also complained much; especially was this the case in respect to the hardships he endured in Missouri; and subsequently of his poverty and illness at Nauvoo. This habit of complaining doubtless did much to deprive him of the Spirit of the Lord; for at times it bordered upon blasphemy. More than once he was heard to say that Jesus Christ was a fool in suffering as compared with himself! (*Succession in the Presidency,* p. 8.)

Sidney was not able to totally bend his will to that of the Lord. In August 1843, Joseph accused Sidney of acts of betrayal and withdrew the hand of fellowship from him. (See *History of the Church,* 5:532.) By October 1843, Joseph said that he had "thrown [Sidney] off his shoulders" and attempted to have him released from the First Presidency. The Prophet indicated that Rigdon had been of little value to him as a counselor since the expulsion from Missouri. However, the conference voted to retain Sidney for yet another year. (See *History of the Church,* 6:47–49.)

The errant first counselor moved to Pittsburgh and was residing there at the time of the Prophet's martyrdom. In residing outside of Nauvoo, he had ignored a revelation from the Lord wherein he was admonished to "locate his family in the neighborhood" where the Prophet Joseph was residing and to "not remove his family unto the eastern lands," away from Nauvoo. (D&C 124:105–10.)

Upon hearing that Joseph Smith had been martyred on June 27, 1844, Rigdon hurried to Nauvoo, arriving there on

August 3. Upon his arrival, he made no effort to confer with the members of the Twelve who were in town—Parley P. Pratt, John Taylor, Willard Richards, and George A. Smith. Instead, he met with William Marks, the local stake president, and began agitating on the issue of succession. He claimed to have received a vision on the day the Prophet was martyred in which he was told that "there must be a guardian appointed to build the church up to Joseph," and claimed that he was the one sent to do that work. (*History of the Church,* 7:224.) He postulated that no man could take Joseph's position as president.

Sidney attempted to get William Marks to call a special conference of the Church for August 6 to discuss the issue of appointing a guardian. He claimed that this needed to be done quickly, for if the people in Nauvoo did not want his leadership, "there was a people numbering thousands and tens of thousands who would receive him" beyond the borders of Nauvoo. (*History of the Church,* 7:225.) There was some opposition to holding a meeting before others of the apostles returned to Nauvoo, and the meeting was providentially postponed until August 8, by which time Brigham Young and a majority of the Twelve had arrived in town.

On the afternoon of August 7, the Twelve called a meeting that included the high council and the high priests. Sidney Rigdon was invited to participate in the meeting and to relay his purported revelation about his appointment as the guardian to the Church. In the course of his comments, he said: "It was shown to me that this church must be built up to Joseph, and that all the blessings we receive must come through him. I have been ordained a spokesman to Joseph, and I must . . . see that the church is governed in a proper manner. Joseph sustains the same relationship to this church as he has always done. No man can be the successor of Joseph." (*History of the Church,* 7:229.)

Brigham Young responded, "I do not care who leads the church, ... but one thing I must know, and that is what God says about it. I have the keys and the means of obtaining the mind of God on the subject." President Young went on to declare: "Joseph conferred upon our heads all the keys and powers belonging to the Apostleship which he himself held before he was taken away, and no man or set of men can get between Joseph and the Twelve in this world or in the world to come. How often has Joseph said to the Twelve, 'I have laid the foundation and you must build thereon, for upon your shoulders the kingdom rests.' " (*History of the Church,* 7:230.)

On the morning of August 8, the Saints in Nauvoo assembled in a special meeting to consider the issue of choosing "a guardian, or President and Trustee." (*History of the Church,* 7:231.) Sidney Rigdon spoke for one and a half hours on the issue, trying to persuade the Saints to support him. The meeting was adjourned and reconvened in the afternoon, under the direction of seven members of the Twelve: Brigham Young, Heber C. Kimball, Parley P. Pratt, Orson Pratt, Willard Richards, Wilford Woodruff, and George A. Smith. John Taylor was confined to his home, recovering from the wounds he received in the attack that took the lives of Joseph and Hyrum Smith. Four other apostles had not yet arrived in Nauvoo.

Brigham Young arose to speak and noted that for the first time in his life and in the lives of the assembled Saints, they were without a prophet at their head. However, he quickly observed that the apostles held "the keys of the kingdom of God in all the world." (*History of the Church,* 7:232.) The spirit of inspiration rested upon the President of the Twelve, and the Lord manifested in a marvelous way to many present that here was indeed the man chosen to lead the people at this time. A transformation seemed to come upon him, and many saw and heard not Brigham Young, but their beloved Prophet Joseph.

One witness of this miraculous outpouring of the Spirit, George Q. Cannon, said:

> If Joseph had risen from the dead, and again spoken in their hearing, the effect could not have been more startling than it was to many present at that meeting; it was the voice of Joseph himself; and not only was it the voice of Joseph which was heard, but it seemed in the eyes of the people as if it was the very person of Joseph which stood before them. A more wonderful and miraculous event than was wrought that day in the presence of that congregation we never heard of. The Lord gave his people a testimony that left no room for doubt, as to who was the man he had chosen to lead them. (In Edward W. Tullidge, *The Life of Brigham Young or, Utah and Her Founders* [New York: n.p., 1877], p. 115; see also Roberts, *Succession in the Presidency,* p. 7.)

President Young issued this warning to those who would seek to lead the people astray: "*All that want to draw away a party from the church after them, let them do it if they can, but they will not prosper.*" He again reminded the Saints that "there is power with the Apostles," for they "are appointed by the finger of God" and "stand next to Joseph, and [now] are as the First Presidency of the Church." A little later, he stated, "We have a head, and that head is the Apostleship." (*History of the Church,* 7:232–33, 235.)

Referring to Elder Rigdon's claims, President Young asked in a vein of humor: "Do you want the church properly organized, or do you want a spokesman to be chief cook and bottle-washer? Elder Rigdon claims to be spokesman to the Prophet. Very well, he was; but can he now act in that office? If he wants now to be a spokesman to the Prophet, he must

go to the other side of the veil, for the Prophet is there."
(*History of the Church,* 7:234.)

Brigham Young's claims were consistent with the stated
position of the Prophet Joseph Smith, who earlier had said:
"Where I am not, there is no First Presidency over the
Twelve." (*Teachings of Joseph Smith,* p. 106.) The death of
the President of the Church automatically released the counselors in the presidency. From June 27, 1844, Sidney Rigdon
held no position in the Church.

At Elder Rigdon's request, rather than voting on his request for guardianship, a vote was first taken to see if the
Saints wanted to uphold and sustain the Twelve as their leaders. The vote was unanimous, and thus the question of Sidney
Rigdon becoming a guardian for the Church became a moot
issue. President Young affirmed his feelings of fellowship for
the former counselor in the First Presidency and said, "We
want such men as Brother Rigdon" to help build the kingdom.
(*History of the Church,* 7:240.)

Publicly, Sidney Rigdon appeared to abide by the voice
of the Saints to support the Twelve Apostles. Yet secretly,
noted B. H. Roberts, Sidney began holding meetings with

> men of questionable integrity in The Church, telling
> them that it was revealed to him before leaving Pittsburg
> that The Church would reject him; but, nevertheless, he
> was the proper person to lead The Church—to be its
> "Guardian;" for to that position he had been called of
> God, and held the keys of authority higher than any
> conferred upon the Prophet Joseph—the keys of David
> which, according to his representations, gave him the
> power to open and no man could shut; to shut and no
> man could open; and the power to organize the armies
> for the destruction of the Gentiles. In fact his fervid
> imagination pictured himself a great military chieftain,
> by whose prowess all the enemies of God were to be

subdued. He secretly ordained men to be prophets, priests and kings to the Gentiles. He also chose and appointed military officers to take command of the armies that were to be raised ere long to fight the battles of the great God. (*Succession in the Presidency,* p. 16.)

The Twelve became aware of Sidney's clandestine activities, and he was called to give an accounting to them. At first he tried to deny his actions, but finally defiantly admitted his actions and challenged the authority of the Twelve, claiming he stood above them. Because of his refusal to repent, a Church disciplinary council was held for Sidney Rigdon on September 8, and he was excommunicated from the Church. (See *History of the Church,* 7:266–69.)

John Taylor noted:

After his excommunication he made an attempt at organizing a church, choosing twelve apostles, etc., but his efforts amounted to but little. He soon retired from Nauvoo to Pittsburg, Pennsylvania, which he established as his headquarters. He sent missionaries to many branches of The Church to represent his claims to the Presidency, but they succeeded in getting only slight support, and that for the most part from among those weak in the faith. His church, never strong either in numbers or prominent men, soon crumbled into decay; Sidney Rigdon himself sank out of sight and in 1876 he died in obscurity in Alleghany County, state of New York. (In *Succession in the Presidency,* pp. 17–18.)

Elder B. H. Roberts commented on Sidney's demise: "The fate of Sidney Rigdon and the fate of the organization which he founded prove the prophetic character of the words of Brigham Young: 'All that want to draw away a party from the church after them, let them do it if they can, but they will not prosper.' " (*Succession in the Presidency,* p. 18.)

James J. Strang

In 1832, a young man imbued with grandiose ideas of personal fame and glory wrote the following in his diary: "I am 19 years old and am yet no more than a common farmer. It is too bad. I ought to have been a member of Assembly or a Brigadier General before this time if I am ever to rival Cesar [sic] or Napoleon which I have sworn to do." (O. W. Riegel, *Crown of Glory* [New Haven: Yale University Press, 1935], p. 12.) This entry in the personal diary of James Jesse Strang gives some insight to the driving force behind the man who twelve years later became a claimant to the mantle of the martyred prophet, Joseph Smith.

He was introduced to the gospel by several of his brothers-in-law and journeyed to Nauvoo where he was baptized on February 25, 1844, just four months before the martyrdom. The Prophet Joseph performed the baptism. One week later Hyrum Smith conferred the Melchizedek Priesthood upon the new convert and ordained him to the office of an elder.

One biographer suggested that "Joseph Smith saw useful material in the well-informed, ambitious, and fluent attorney, for . . . [James Strang] became at once an active and trusted member of the Mormon ministry. His special field of labor was Wisconsin, and he soon applied for authority to there 'plant a stake of Zion.' " (Charles K. Backus, *The King of Beaver Island* [Los Angeles: Westernlore Press, 1955], pp. 19–20.)

While in Wisconsin, Strang claimed to have been visited by an angel on the day that the Prophet was martyred. He said that the heavenly messenger "stretched forth his hand unto him and touched his head, and put oil upon him." This newcomer to Mormonism claimed that he was to be "the supreme ruler of the Saints on earth." (*Crown of Glory,* p. 31.) Although Strang later wrote down the five hundred and seven words he alleged that the angel said to him, it is of interest to note that not one of those words mentioned the slain prophet of the Church.

Strang's most significant claim to the leadership of the Church was based on a letter he purportedly received from the Prophet Joseph, dated June 18, 1844. In that letter Joseph is alleged to have related a vision he had in which James J. Strang was appointed as Joseph's successor to lead the Saints, for "to him shall the gathering of the people be." Strang also claimed that the vision instructed him to establish a stake and build a house of the Lord in Wisconsin in a city to be known as Voree. The letter closed with these words: "If evil befall me thou shalt lead the flock to pleasant pastures. God sustain thee." (*Restoration Reporter* 1, no. 1 (Dec. 1970): 3; original letter in the Coe Collection at Yale University.)

There are a number of questionable facets about this alleged letter from the Prophet. Only the signature of the letter appeared to be in Joseph Smith's handwriting. In addition, the letter was initially kept secret from the public, and the only one claiming to know of its existence was Strang's brother-in-law, Aaron Smith, who coincidentally was mentioned in the letter as one to be called as a counselor to Strang. The postmark on the letter also had some questionable aspects. Furthermore, the register that would have shown what letters came from Nauvoo to the local post office mysteriously disappeared before it could be proven whether or not the letter had passed through the post office. (See *Crown of Glory*, pp. 32–35.)

Rather than take his claim of authority to the center of the Church in Nauvoo, Strang went to Florence, Michigan, where on August 5 he read the letter to an assembled group of members and requested their sustaining vote in his behalf. When asked if he had been ordained as Joseph's successor, Strang replied that he had not and that it was not necessary. Significantly, he did not mention his alleged "anointing" by the angel on June 27. It was only several months later that he made this claim known, after being informed that a revelation from the Lord outlined the necessity of one's being properly ordained. (See D&C 42:11.)

Strang angrily stalked out of the Florence conference when his authority was challenged. "It is not my understanding," he said, "that Elders exercise discipline over the First President." His claims had an unsettling influence on those in attendance, for the following resolution was passed: "Those of the elders who were satisfied with the evidence of his calling, might proclaim it, taking upon themselves the responsibility in case it should prove an error, and those who were not satisfied should say nothing on the subject till further directions." (*Crown of Glory*, pp. 36–37.)

Elder Crandall Dunn, the presiding elder in Florence, excommunicated Strang from the Church and sent a report to the Twelve Apostles at Nauvoo. The Twelve, in turn, as the presiding officers of the Church, excommunicated Strang and his fellow claimant to authority, Aaron Smith, in August of 1844.

Strang sought to strengthen his assertion to authority by duplicating some of the events that occurred in Joseph Smith's life. In September of 1845, Strang laid claim to having been visited by an angel who told him of some buried plates that had been reserved for him to discover and translate. Four of his followers, including Aaron Smith, purportedly uncovered the plates and signed an affidavit testifying to that effect.

One biographer wrote the following regarding Strang's attempt to duplicate the Prophet Joseph Smith's bringing forth of the plates from which the Book of Mormon was translated: "As Joseph found in the Ontario hills a golden volume in which the chronicles of the Book of Mormon were preserved in cabalistic characters, translatable only by the crystalline Urim and Thummim, so James discovered in the sloping banks of the White River a long-buried and miraculously preserved record of the downfall of a great Israelitish tribe which inhabited this continent centuries ago, and whose patriarch, in lamenting the annihilation of his people, foretold the coming in future ages of a 'mighty prophet,' who 'should bring forth the record.' " (*King of Beaver Island,* p. 23.)

Four years after his "discovery" of the plates at White River in Walworth County, Wisconsin, Strang claimed to have received "the 18–plates of Laban," a direct reference to the brass plates mentioned in the Book of Mormon. His translation of these plates, together with several of his contemporary revelations, formed his publication of The Book of the Law of the Lord. In imitation of the Latter-day Saint's publication of the Doctrine and Covenants, Strang had seven witnesses sign their names to a testimonial page at the front of his latest publication.

Strang was innovative, and his charismatic personality attracted a number of followers to his false fold. Centuries before, the Savior had warned of "false prophets [who] shall rise, and shall shew signs and wonders, to seduce, if it were possible, even the elect." (Mark 13:22.)

Among those who followed James Strang at some point during his abortive ministry were some of the "elect," such as William Smith and John E. Page of the Quorum of the Twelve; former apostle William E. M'Lellin, who was excommunicated in 1838; and William Marks, Nauvoo Stake president. In addition, Strang's followers included such prominent rogues as John C. Bennett, whom the historian Bancroft described as having ability and brains, "but no soul." (In B. H. Roberts, *Comprehensive History of The Church of Jesus Christ of Latter-day Saints,* 6 vols. [Provo, Utah: The Church of Jesus Christ of Latter-day Saints, 1930], 2:47.) Bennett, who had been excommunicated in 1842, endeared himself to Strang by referring to the latter as "the Imperial Primate over all Israel" and claimed for himself the position of "General-in-Chief." (*Crown of Glory,* p. 75.) All of these men eventually had a falling out with Strang, and some ended up in the movement that ultimately became the Reorganized Church of Jesus Christ of Latter Day Saints.

Strang led his followers to establish the "cornerstone of Zion" on Beaver Island, one of twelve in a cluster in Lake Michigan. He renamed the harbor city after himself, calling it St. James, and was recklessly hostile to any who did not accept him as their prophet-leader. He had himself crowned as king of the island and began to amass great political power in the area. But he also had many detractors, some of them quite acrid in their feelings toward him. James J. Strang was shot by an assailant on June 16, 1856, and died on July 9. His church essentially fell into disarray, although one might find a few followers of his teachings even in our day.

Perhaps a good summary of Strang's claim to authority is found in the following note written to this pretended leader by two of the Twelve Apostles whom Strang had challenged to a debate on the issue of authority: "Sir — After Lucifer was cut off and thrust down to hell, we have no knowledge that God condescended to investigate the subject or right of authority with him. Your case has been disposed of by the authorities of The Church. Being satisfied with our own power and calling, we have no disposition to ask from whence yours came. Respectfully, Orson Hyde, John Taylor." (*Succession in the Presidency,* p. 36, note.)

Alpheus Cutler

Although he was a minor character in the drama that ensued on the issue of succession, Alpheus Cutler was one of those who claimed to have been secretly ordained as Joseph Smith's successor. Cutler played an active role in the Church during its formative years, serving on high councils and other special committees, including the Council of Fifty. (The Council of Fifty, which included non-Mormons, was organized to relieve the First Presidency and the Twelve of temporal responsibilities, especially in political and economic planning.)

His actions following the martyrdom indicate that he initially supported the Twelve Apostles. He received his endowments in the Nauvoo Temple in December 1845 and was called to serve as a captain of one of the pioneer companies heading west. Although he started on the journey, he later withdrew from the main body of the Saints and established a colony of followers in Iowa. He was excommunicated from the Church on April 20, 1851, and formed his own apostate organization, "The True Church of Jesus Christ," on September 19, 1853. (See Brewster, *Encyclopedia,* p. 118.)

His claims to authority were described in an official history of his church:

> Joseph Smith, sometime prior to his death, organized a Quorum of Seven, all of whom were ordained under his hand to the prophetic office; with all the rights, keys, powers, privileges, and blessings belonging to that condition. The only difference in the ordination of the seven, was in the case of Alpheus Cutler, whose right to act as prophet, seer, and revelator was to be in force upon the whole world from that very hour. Under this ordination, he claimed an undisputed right to organize and build up the kingdom the same as Joseph Smith had done. (Chancey Whiting, Sr., quoted in Rupert J. Fletcher and Daisy Whiting Fletcher, *Alpheus Cutler and the Church of Jesus Christ* [Independence, Missouri: The Church of Jesus Christ, 1974], p. 53.)

Alpheus Cutler was sustained by his followers as "our head or chief Councilor," and another man was appointed as the president of the organization. His organization reached a peak of 183 members by 1859, but gradually declined to a handful of followers. (Diary of William W. Blair, 1863–64, 13 March 1863, RLDS Archives; cited in Quinn, "The Mormon Succession Crisis," p. 198.)

William Smith

Another of the claimants to the presiding position of the Church was Joseph Smith's younger brother William. He was one of the original apostles chosen in February of 1835. However, his headstrong attitude often put him at odds with the Prophet and his brethren among the Twelve. He was aware of his weaknesses, and in December of 1835, following a public disagreement with Joseph and Hyrum, he suggested that it might be best to be released from his apostolic calling. William said:

> It would be better for [the apostles] to appoint one, in the office, that would be better able to fill [the office], and by doing this they would . . . leave me where I was before I was chosen; then I would not be in a situation to bring so much disgrace upon the cause, when I fall into temptation; and perhaps, by this I might obtain salvation. You know my passions and the danger of falling from so high a station; and thus by withdrawing from the office of the Apostleship, while there is salvation for me, and remaining a member of the Church—I feel afraid, if I don't do this, it will be worse for me some other day. (*History of the Church,* 2:339.)

In responding to his brother's request, the Prophet referred to William's "passions" as "that wicked spirit." (*History of the Church,* 2:342.) In Joseph's response to his brother's request to be released from his calling among the Twelve, much can be learned about serving faithfully:

> You desire to remain in the Church, but forsake

your Apostleship. This is the stratagem of the evil one; when he has gained one advantage, he lays a plan for another. But by maintaining your Apostleship, in rising up and making one tremendous effort, you may overcome your passions and please God. And by forsaking your Apostleship, is not to be willing to make that sacrifice that God requires at your hands, and is to incur His displeasure; and without pleasing God, we do not think it will be any better for you. When a man falls one step, he must regain that step again, or fall another; he has still more to gain, or eventually all is lost. (*History of the Church*, 2:342–43.)

William retained his office, but his "passions" got him in continuing difficulties, and in 1839 he was dropped from the Quorum of the Twelve for a three-week period.

He received the keys of the kingdom along with his brethren of the Twelve under the hands of Joseph Smith prior to the martyrdom of his brothers, the Prophet and the Patriarch. He sustained the right of the Twelve to lead the Church following the deaths of Joseph and Hyrum Smith. In a published statement on May 15, 1845, he said: "My advice to all, without respect of persons, is the same now that it was then. Support and uphold the proper authorities of the church—when I say authorities, I mean the whole, and not a part; the *Twelve,* and not one, two, six, eight, ten or eleven, but the whole *Twelve;* follow me as I follow Christ, God being our judge." (In *Times and Seasons* 6:904.)

Being the eldest surviving son of the Patriarch Joseph Smith, Sr., William was ordained the Patriarch to the Church on May 24, 1845, which office he held in addition to his apostolic calling. Because of a misprint in a Church publication that announced his calling as Patriarch "over" the Church, William claimed precedence over the Twelve. Although he reaffirmed his support of the Twelve in July of that same year, his rebellious spirit led the Saints to fail to sustain him either as an apostle or as the Patriarch on October 6, 1845. He published a pamphlet against the Twelve and was excommunicated on October 19, 1845.

William apparently did not have the ability to attract much of a following to his own claims to authority, and he became affiliated with several splinter groups over the next few years. In 1846 he joined Strang's organization as a patriarch but left a year later amid much bitterness. He unsuccessfully attempted to gather a group of Saints at Palestine Grove, Illinois, in 1848 and finally effected a new organization at Covington, Kentucky, in 1850 based on the doctrine of lineal descent. William served as "president pro tem," with former quorum member Lyman Wight as one of his counselors. Jason Briggs, one of the key figures in the later organization of the Reorganized Church, served as a member of William's council of apostles. This organization did not last, and William later became nominally affiliated with the Reorganized movement. (See Russell Rich, *Those Who Would Be Leaders* [Provo: Brigham Young University Press, 1967], pp. 40–42.)

Lyman Wight

Lyman Wight was ordained an apostle by Joseph Smith on April 8, 1841. During the trying days of Missouri, Lyman had proven himself a faithful defender of the faith and of its prophet-leader, who nicknamed him the "wild ram of the mountains." Following the death of the Prophet Joseph, Elder Wight found it difficult to bend his will to that of the entire Twelve.

Evidently as a member of Joseph's Council of Fifty, Elder Wight had been commissioned by Joseph Smith to establish a colony in Texas. The Texas mission became Wight's singular focus, and he rebelled against his associates in the Twelve, claiming that the Council of Fifty had a higher authority than the apostles. He argued that the Saints should go to Texas and establish themselves in that area of the country rather than go west as Brigham Young counseled. In 1845 he led a small colony to Texas. He was excommunicated by the Twelve on December 3, 1848, and the following year became a counselor to William Smith in the latter's organization. Wight espoused the idea of lineal succession and promoted Joseph Smith III as the rightful successor to his illustrious father.

In spite of this, however, Wight claimed personal authority by secret ordination from the Prophet Joseph. In July 1855, Wight wrote that he had been ordained to the office of "Benamey" in 1834 in the presence of an angel. He further claimed that Joseph had given him a lifelong mission in 1844: "The revolation of the Lord was given by the angel of the seventh dispensation and was to continue during my life it was given by the highest authority that then was and I can not see any use or benefit it could be to alter it especially as their is no power on earth that can do it. . . . my mission was to continue dureing my life and as Joseph never found fault with me and no other man has authority to do so I think my case will lay over till the Lord takes me to himself." (Letterbook of Lyman Wight, Research Library and Archives, RLDS Church, p. 25; cited in Quinn, "The Mormon Succession Crisis," p. 197.)

Wight did not claim presiding authority over the Church, for at various times he supported different individuals or groups. However, he did claim that "no other man" had authority over him; he was independent of all others. His followers quickly dispersed following his death in 1858.

John E. Page

Elder John E. Page was the first man to be ordained as a replacement for one of the original apostles called in 1835.

He received his ordination on December 19, 1838, being ordained under the hands of Brigham Young and Heber C. Kimball. Unfortunately, he did not remain true. Like others who ultimately fell away from the Church, Elder Page displayed an independence that made it difficult for him to humble himself before proper authority.

In 1836 he was called on a mission to Canada but initially declined because he said he didn't have the means. Joseph Smith took the coat off his own back and gave it to the reluctant missionary, promising him success and the the Lord's blessings. In 1840 he was called to go on a mission to Palestine with fellow apostle Orson Hyde, but he failed to do so.

In April 1843, he organized a branch in Cincinnati with a constitution requiring the branch president to be elected every four years. Several months later Elders Heber C. Kimball and Orson Pratt reorganized the branch and its policies according to accepted Church procedures. Upon their departure from the area, Elder Page immediately reinstated his previous policies and changed the branch leadership. This action was overturned by Elders Brigham Young, Wilford Woodruff, and George A. Smith, who visited the branch shortly thereafter.

Although he had initially publicly endorsed the right of the Twelve Apostles to lead the Church following the death of the Prophet, his rebellious spirit led him to break with the Twelve. He took out an advertisement in a newspaper, which Andrew Jensen noted suggested that he "was out of employment and would preach for anybody that would sustain his family." (*LDS Biographical Encyclopedia,* 4 vols. [Salt Lake City: Western Epics, 1971], 1:93.)

John E. Page was disfellowshipped from the Quorum of the Twelve on February 9, 1846. He then joined with the Strang movement, offering his services "to let loos[e] my small artillery in a war of *words* against false principles." (*Crown of Glory,* p. 68.) On his way to Wisconsin to join with Strang, Page met a company of Saints coming from Canada. He claimed authority to lead them to Wisconsin. A few were deceived, but the majority continued on to Nauvoo to join the main body of the Saints under the direction of the Twelve Apostles. He was excommunicated on June 26, 1846. (See Melvin R. Brooks, *LDS Reference Encyclopedia,* 2 vols. [Salt Lake City: Bookcraft, 1960–65], 1:359.) One biographer noted that John E. Page's "apostolic title, 'The Sun Dial,' was curiously appropriate, for like a sun dial, he marked only the sunny hours." (*Crown of Glory,* p. 68.)

David Whitmer

Of all the false claimants to presiding authority following Joseph Smith's death, David Whitmer was the one who really had some historical basis on which to base his claim. As noted in the previous chapter, David had at one time been designated by the Prophet himself as his successor. However, this designation was later changed: First, by Oliver Cowdery's subsequent and superseding ordination as the Associate President of the Church, which placed the Prophet's former scribe in the role of successor to the President. And second, David Whitmer's excommunication in 1838, which not only deprived him of Church membership but of his priesthood authority as well.

Following his excommunication, David Whitmer remained in Missouri for the next fifty years of his life. Three years after the martyrdom of Joseph Smith, the excommunicated and former apostle William E. M'Lellin induced David to join a movement he had organized. On February 10, 1847, David Whitmer was sustained as the president of this new church, which was called "The Church of Christ."

A schism arose between Whitmer and M'Lellin, partly

because the designated president refused to move from his home in Richmond, Missouri, to Kirtland, Ohio, which M'Lellin wanted as the headquarters for his church. David broke from the church, confessing, as Richard L. Anderson said, "that he had been emotionally moved instead of divinely directed" to join with M'Lellin. He appeared to be embarrassed about this brief association. ("David Whitmer, the Independent Missouri Businessman," *Improvement Era,* April 1969, p. 76; William E. Berrett, *The Restored Church,* 11th ed. [Salt Lake City: Deseret Book, 1963], p. 209.)

In a letter dated July 28, 1847, Oliver Cowdery, David's fellow witness of the Book of Mormon, wrote to his friend regarding keys of priesthood authority. "Now whether the Lord will call us again publicly or not to work in his great cause, is not known to me," declared Oliver. "We may not live to see the day," he continued, "but *we have the authority.* AND DO HOLD THE KEYS. It is important, should we not be permitted to act in that authority, that we confer them upon some man or men, whom God may appoint, that this priesthood be not taken again from the earth." (*Ensign of Liberty* 1, no. 6 [May 1848]: 92.)

Evidently neither Oliver nor David understood that keys of priesthood authority do not remain with one who has been excommunicated from the Church by those who are in authority. Or perhaps they did not feel that their excommunications were completely valid. They also did not seem to understand, at least at that time, that these keys had been bestowed upon the Twelve Apostles. Shortly after he wrote this letter, Oliver evidently gained an understanding of these principles because he was rebaptized into The Church of Jesus Christ of Latter-day Saints on November 12, 1848, and affirmed his support of the Twelve Apostles as the legal and rightful holders of the keys of priesthood authority.

Both publicly and privately Oliver Cowdery declared that

"the 'Twelve' were the only men that could lead the Church after the death of Joseph, and that every man that wished to do right would follow the main channel of the stream." When later questioned about the contents of his letter to David Whitmer, Oliver replied: "When I wrote that letter I did not know of the revelation which says, that the keys and power conferred upon me, were taken from me and placed upon the head of Hyrum Smith [see D&C 124:91–95], and it was that revelation which changed my views on this subject." He went on to say that he was not seeking position in the Church but merely to once again become a member thereof and that he had no "pretensions to authority." (Junius F. Wells, "Oliver Cowdery," *Improvement Era,* March 1911, pp. 393–94.)

Unfortunately, David Whitmer did not follow the same path of return as Oliver Cowdery. In 1876 he ordained a nephew to "organize a new church according to the original pattern." Not much came of this or of another feeble effort to organize a church several years before his death. (Quinn, "The Mormon Succession Crisis," p. 209; Berrett, *The Restored Church,* p. 209.)

In April 1887, David Whitmer published a booklet entitled "An Address to All Believers in Christ by a Witness to the Divine Authenticity of the Book of Mormon." The title, of course, bore continued witness of his firm belief in the divine manifestation that had been his, but the contents exhibited his differences with the divine Church of which he had been an original member. While never denying his testimony of the Book of Mormon, David died in 1888 outside the Church that held the priesthood authority necessary to provide him the ordinances of salvation.

William Marks

Although he did not hold apostolic keys, William Marks was in a position of power and prominence at the time of the martrydoms of Joseph and Hyrum Smith. Marks was the president of the Nauvoo Stake and, as pointed out earlier, was the one to whom Sidney Rigdon first went in his aborted attempt to become the guardian for the Church. While he was sympathetic to Rigdon's cause, William Marks initially sustained the Twelve Apostles in their rightful role as the ones who should lead the Church following the August 1844 meeting in Nauvoo.

By October he was found to be in rebellion against the leadership of the Twelve and was rejected as the Nauvoo Stake president, with only two members voting to sustain him. He repented for a time and published the following statement on December 9, 1844: "After mature and candid deliberation, I am fully and satisfactorily convinced that Mr. Sidney Rigdon's claims to the presidency of the church of Jesus Christ of Latter-day Saints, are not founded in truth. I have been deceived by his specious pretenses and now feel to warn every one over whom I have any influence to beware of him and his pretended visions and revelations. The Twelve are the proper persons to lead the church." (*Times and Seasons* 5:742.)

The former stake president of Nauvoo did not remain true to the Twelve and was excommunicated in 1845. He joined the Strangite movement and presided over one of this group's conferences, held on April 6, 1846, in which James J. Strang was sustained as their prophet. During a three-year period with Strang's church, Marks served as president of the high priests quorum, bishop, apostle, and as a member of the First Presidency.

He became disaffected with Strang and in 1852 joined a movement established by Charles B. Thompson, who had followed the Strangites for a time before breaking to establish his own organization. Thompson claimed to be "Baneemy, patriarch of Zion." (Leonard J. Arrington and Davis Bitton,

The Mormon Experience [New York: Alfred Knopf, 1979], p. 90.) Marks was called by Thompson to find a suitable gathering place for the Saints. The wanderlust hit Marks again, and he left Thompson's group. Then in 1855 he joined an organization established by John E. Page.

In 1859, this former rock of Nauvoo, now turned rolling stone, joined the movement that became the Reorganized Church. He was allowed into this organization on the basis of his original baptism in The Church of Jesus Christ of Latter-day Saints, the Church from which he had been excommunicated fifteen years earlier.

In April of 1860, Marks helped "ordain" Joseph Smith III as the president and prophet of the Reorganized Church of Jesus Christ of Latter Day Saints. He became first counselor in the First Presidency of this organization and served in that capacity until his death in 1872.

The Reorganized Movement

Of all the splinter groups that broke from the the leadership of the Twelve Apostles, only one has sustained any substantial following over the years. The Reorganized Church of Jesus Christ of Latter Day Saints had its beginnings in 1852 when Jason W. Briggs and Zenas (sometimes spelled Zenos) H. Gurley formed the "New Organization" from several branches of Strang's church. Joseph Fielding Smith estimated that this new group included about 100 members, "most of whom were converts made for Mr. Strang." (*Doctrines of Salvation*, 1:252.)

Jason Briggs had joined The Church of Jesus Christ of Latter-day Saints in 1841 and remained in the Church under the leadership of the Twelve Apostles until 1846. He did not follow the main body of the Saints to the West, remaining behind where he eventually joined James J. Strang's movement. He served as a missionary for Strang in 1848. He renounced Strang in 1850 and accepted William Smith's claims, becoming an apostle in this new church.

Briggs claimed to have received a revelation in 1851 wherein he was convinced that William Smith was wrong in his claims and that "in the Lord's own due time He would call upon the seed of Joseph Smith to preside over the high priesthood of the Church." (Samuel H. Carpenter, "Facts about Differences That Persist between the Reorganized Church of Jesus Christ of Latter Day Saints and The Church of Jesus Christ of Latter-day Saints" [The Hague, Holland: Netherlands Mission of The Church of Jesus Christ of Latter-day Saints, 1959], p. 7.)

Zenas Gurley joined The Church of Jesus Christ of Latter-day Saints in 1838 and held the office of seventy at the time of the martyrdom. He supported the Twelve Apostles until the time of the exodus from Nauvoo. He left the Church and joined with James J. Strang, filling a mission for this self-proclaimed prophet. In 1852 Gurley claimed to have received a revelation designating Joseph Smith III as the one who should rightfully lead the Saints.

Both Briggs and Gurley became two of the seven apostles chosen in 1853 to lead this new organization, with Briggs presiding as the senior officer, where he remained until 1860. The revelation to choose the apostles and a provisional president originated with H. H. Deam, who was one of the seven chosen to fill the presiding positions in the new organization. The presidency of the new organization was offered to the son of Joseph and Emma Smith, Joseph Smith III, but the youth initially declined the offer. Deam claimed that because the Prophet's son had "neglected to comply with the will of God," he "had forfeited the right, and that it was our privilege and duty to go forward and fully organize." ("Facts about Differences," p. 13.) Deam and John Cunningham, another of the seven apostles, were expelled from the quorum for promoting this idea.

In 1860, twenty-eight-year-old Joseph Smith III accepted the presidency of what is now known as the Reorganized Church of Jesus Christ of Latter Day Saints. He was ordained as "President of the high priesthood and president of the church" under the hands of four men: William Marks, Zenas Gurley, Samuel Powers, and W. W. Blair. (*The Restored Church,* p. 210.) Regarding the authority of these four men to perform this ordination, one should consider the word of the Lord revealed in 1831: "It shall not be given to any one to go forth to preach my gospel, or to build up my church, except he be ordained by some one who has authority, and it is known to the church that he has authority and has been regularly ordained by the heads of the church." (D&C 42:11.)

Neither Samuel Powers nor W. W. Blair ever held priesthood or membership in the Church established by the Lord through the Prophet Joseph Smith during his lifetime, which church is "the only true and living church upon the face of the whole earth." (D&C 1:30.) As previously indicated, William Marks and Zenas Gurley both initially sustained the Twelve Apostles as the rightful leaders of the Church and kingdom of God on earth, but both later fell away and followed several offshoot organizations. Whence did their authority come? For a thorough discussion on this matter, one might study *Origin of the Reorganized Church and the Question of Succession* by Elder Joseph Fielding Smith.

It is of interest to note that Briggs left the Reorganization in 1886, repudiating the fundamental doctrines of the church he had helped organize. He was joined in his departure by the family of his fellow founder, Zenas Gurley.

The Reorganized Church was based essentially on the doctrine of lineal succession, or the right of presidency passing from father to son. From 1860 until the early 1990s, the Reorganites have followed this line of succession. Three of Joseph Smith III's sons followed their father in the presidency

(Frederick M. Smith, Israel A. Smith, and W. Wallace Smith). One grandson, Wallace B. Smith, came to the presidency in 1978. However, this last president has no sons to follow him in office. Thus, the basic principle upon which the Reorganization was founded can no longer be followed.

In addition to the right of presidency through lineal succession, the Reorganized movement has taken issue with The Church of Jesus Christ of Latter-day Saints on other issues like plural marriage, plurality of gods, baptism for the dead, temple ordinances, the literal gathering of the Saints, and granting of the priesthood to women. "Thus," says one source, "the Reorganization came to occupy a stance between standard Protestantism and Utah Mormonism. It retained a belief in a reopened canon, but its doctrinal position edged closer to a socially conscious, conservative sort of Protestantism." (*The Mormon Experience,* pp. 92–93.) As changes have continued in the Reorganized Church, it has continued to move further from the roots from which it claims its authority.

Conclusion

Only a few of the more prominent movements or individuals who have claimed authority to lead the Saints of God have been dealt with in this chapter. From the dissident movement of Wycam Clark's Pure Church of Christ, organized in 1831, up to the present day, there have been many who have severed themselves from the True Tree established by the Lord with its priesthood roots. Some of these hundreds of offshoots have been little known, while others have gained some degree of notoriety through their actions or doctrines.

Brigham Young's pronouncement of August 8, 1844, remains in effect: *"All that want to draw away a party from the church after them, let them do it if they can, but they will not prosper."* (*History of the Church,* 7:232.)

Chapter Five

A Historical Overview of Succession

Brigham Young as the Senior Apostle

As soon as Joseph Smith's spirit took flight from his mortal body, the authority to lead the Church passed to the Twelve Apostles, with Brigham Young as their president. There was no lapse of authority in the interim following the martyrdoms of Joseph and Hyrum Smith on June 27, 1844, and the conference of August 8 where the Twelve were officially sustained in their presiding position over the Church. God knew who His next prophet was even though many in and out of the Church may have been unclear on the issue.

Elder Bruce R. McConkie gave the following testimony of the transition of authority following the martyrdom: "When Joseph Smith — sent to a martyr's death by evil and murderous men — gasps his last breath, Brigham Young, being the next senior officer in the earthly kingdom, automatically becomes its presiding officer. The next breath drawn by Brother Brigham is the breath of power filling the lungs of *the Lord's previously anointed servant*. There is not so long a time as the twinkling of an eye when the Church is without a presiding officer." ("The Keys of the Kingdom," *Ensign*, May 1983, p. 23; italics added.)

Brigham Young and his fellow apostles led the Church as a quorum for a time and did not immediately proceed to reorganize the First Presidency. In an editorial in the Church's official publication, the *Times and Seasons*, dated September 2, 1844, the leaders responded to the question of who would succeed Joseph as President of the Church:

> Great excitement prevails throughout the world to know "who shall be the successor of Joseph Smith?"
>
> In reply, we say, be patient, *be patient* a little, till the proper time comes, and we will tell you all. "Great wheels move slow." At present, we can say that a special conference of the church was held in Nauvoo on the 8th [of August], and it was carried *without a dissenting voice,* that the "Twelve" should preside over the whole church, and when any alteration in the presidency shall be required, seasonable notice will be given; and the elders abroad, will best exhibit their wisdom to all men, by remaining silent on those things they are ignorant of. (5:632.)

Perhaps the Church needed time to make the adjustment from following *the* Prophet of the Restoration to following his successor. Maybe a waiting period wherein twelve men led the Church helped to foil any plans of further assassinations of Church leaders. Whatever the reasons may have been for not immediately reorganizing the presidency of the Church, it is evident that the Lord placed His stamp of approval on this interim of apostolic presidency.

The title of "President of the Church" was attached to Brigham Young several years before the First Presidency was officially reorganized. In a letter dated December 5, 1844, Brigham Young signed himself as "Prest of the Church of

L.D.S." He was "publicly sustained to that position on 7 April 1845, and by 1846 rank-and-file Mormons were referring to Brigham Young as President of the Church." ("The Mormon Succession Crisis," pp. 216, 218.)

On November 15, 1847, the issue of organizing a separate First Presidency was discussed by the Quorum of the Twelve. There was no question about President Young's presiding position, but evidently some among the Twelve wondered whether a separate quorum of three presiding high priests (the First Presidency) was necessary. Brigham Young apparently felt that continuing to have the Twelve preside over the Church required that a majority of them remain at Church headquarters rather than be out in the nations of the world. A First Presidency of three would solve this dilemma.

A number of meetings were held to discuss the matter, culminating with a five-hour meeting on December 5, 1847. President Young said he had "been stirred up to do this by the spirit of the Lord," and the apostles voted to sustain his desire to form a separate First Presidency. In a later private meeting of the apostles, the voice of the Lord ratified the action by declaring: "Let my servant Brigham step forth and receive the full power of the presiding Priesthood in my Church and kingdom." (*Journal of Discourses,* 8:234.)

At a December 27, 1847 Church conference, a constituent body of the Church sustained a separate First Presidency, with Brigham Young as President and fellow apostles Heber C. Kimball and Willard Richards as counselors. Apparently President Young believed the presidency to be an extension of the Quorum of the Twelve. In 1865, almost eighteen years after the First Presidency had been reorganized, Brigham Young declared that "the Twelve have dictated, guided and directed the destinies of this great people" since Joseph Smith's martyrdom. (*Journal of Discourses,* 11:115.)

President Young added additional counselors in the First

Presidency during his administration. Joseph F. Smith was set apart as a counselor to the First Presidency on July 1, 1866. Lorenzo Snow, Brigham Young, Jr., Albert Carrington, John W. Young, and George Q. Cannon were all sustained as additional counselors to Brigham Young on April 8, 1873, and as assistant counselors on May 9, 1874.

During his presidency, Brigham Young also ordained men to the apostolic office independent of the Council of the Twelve. Jedediah M. Grant was ordained an apostle on April 7, 1854, and called to serve as second counselor in the First Presidency. Ten-year-old John W. Young was ordained an apostle by his father on February 22, 1855, and was later called to serve in the First Presidency, where he was the first counselor at the time of President Young's death. He was sustained as a counselor to the Twelve Apostles on October 6, 1877, and released on October 6, 1891. Daniel H. Wells was ordained an apostle on January 4, 1857, and set apart as the second counselor in the First Presidency. He, like John Young, was sustained as a counselor to the Twelve Apostles on October 6, 1877, and served in that capacity until his death in 1891. President Young also ordained two other sons to the apostolic office: Joseph A. Young and Brigham Young, Jr., were both ordained apostles on February 4, 1864. Brigham Young's namesake was ultimately called to serve in the Quorum of the Twelve along with one other apostle ordained outside the quorum — Joseph F. Smith, who was ordained an apostle on July 1, 1866. The significant relationship of apostolic seniority of these two men will be discussed later in this chapter. (See *Deseret News 1987 Church Almanac* [Salt Lake City: Deseret News Press, 1988], pp. 44–49.)

John Taylor as the Senior Apostle

At the death of Brigham Young on August 29, 1877, the First Presidency was dissolved, and the leadership of the

Church devolved upon the Quorum of the Twelve Apostles. At the first general conference of the Church following the death of Brigham Young, his two former counselors were both sustained as counselors to the Twelve Apostles, but, as noted above, neither one was ever set apart as a member of that governing body.

John Taylor was the senior apostle and was sustained as the President of the Twelve Apostles at the October conference in 1877. Regarding his position, President Taylor said: "I occupied the senior position in the quorum, and occupying that position, which was thoroughly understood by the Quorum of the Twelve, on the death of President Young, as the Twelve assumed the presidency, and I was their president, *it placed me in a position of president of the Church.*" (In John A. Widtsoe, *Priesthood and Church Government* [Salt Lake City: Deseret Book, 1939], p. 249; italics added.)

Note that at the time of his being sustained as the senior apostle, three other Apostles were still living and functioning as members of the quorum who had previously been recognized as being senior to John Taylor. Two of these apostles, Orson Hyde and Orson Pratt, were original members of the Twelve selected by the Three Witnesses in 1835. The other, Wilford Woodruff, was called to the apostleship at the same time as Elder Taylor in 1838. (See D&C 118:6.)

Why were none of these men sustained as the presiding officer at the time of Brigham Young's death? An investigation of the facts reveals an important principle of seniority and succession.

When the first twelve men were called to the Quorum of the Twelve Apostles in 1835, there appeared to be little concern about who was senior. In a conference of May 2, 1835, Joseph Smith placed the twelve in a rotating presidency according to age. The Prophet instructed that "it would be the duty of the Twelve, when in council, to take their seats together according to age, the oldest to be seated at the head, and preside in the first council, the next oldest in the second, and so on until the youngest had presided; and then begin at the oldest again." (*History of the Church,* 2:219–20.) Age was the determining factor of seniority.

Because he was the older of the two, Wilford Woodruff was given initial seniority over John Taylor after each had been ordained to fill vacancies in the Quorum of the Twelve. Although they were called on the same day in July of 1838, John Taylor was ordained on December 19, 1838, and Wilford Woodruff on April 26, 1839. For over twenty-two years, Elder Woodruff was seated senior to Elder Taylor.

At the October conference in 1861, Brigham Young directed the clerk of the conference to change the order of seniority involving the two men. He indicated that an apostle's seniority should be based in accordance with the date of his ordination. He indicated that "he spoke of it now because the time would come when a dispute might arise about it." (History of Brigham Young, manuscript, October 1861, p. 437.)

John Taylor gave the following explanation:

> Through some inadvertence, or perhaps mixed up with the idea of seniority of age taking the precedence, Wilford Woodruff's name was placed on the records of the time, and for many years after, before that of John Taylor. This matter was investigated some time afterwards by President Young and his council, sanctioned also by the Twelve, whether John Taylor held the precedency and stood in gradation prior to Brother Wilford Woodruff, and it was voted on and decided that his name be placed before Wilford Woodruff's, although Wilford Woodruff was the older man. The reason assigned for this change was that although both were called at the same time, John Taylor was ordained into the Twelve

81

prior to Wilford Woodruff; and another prominent reason would be that as John Taylor assisted in the ordination of Elder Wilford Woodruff, he therefore must precede him in the Council. (*Succession in the Priesthood* [Salt Lake City: n.p., 1881], p. 16.)

Thus the principle of date and order of ordination as an apostle became a guiding principle in seniority. But what about Elders Hyde and Pratt? Both were ordained prior to John Taylor.

In October of 1838, Orson Hyde got caught up in some of the criticism leveled at the Prophet Joseph Smith and the Church. Being "overcome by the spirit of darkness" (Smith, *Essentials in Church History,* p. 289), he signed an affidavit supporting false and inflammatory accusations against the Church by apostate Thomas B. Marsh. Elder Hyde was dropped from the Quorum of the Twelve on May 4, 1839, but repented and returned to activity in the Church the following month. On June 27, he was reinstated in the quorum where he took his original place of seniority. When Brigham Young, Heber C. Kimball, and Willard Richards were sustained as the First Presidency on December 27, 1847, Orson Hyde was sustained as the President of the Twelve Apostles. He served in this position until 1875, at which time Brigham Young placed John Taylor ahead of Elder Hyde.

Because of a gross misunderstanding, believing the false accusations of an apostate rather than the words of the Prophet of God, both Orson Pratt and his wife were excommunicated from the Church on August 20, 1842. (See Ivan J. Barrett, *Joseph Smith and the Restoration* [Provo: Brigham Young University Press, 1973], pp. 523–24.) Within six months Orson had resolved his differences and recognized the falseness of the accusations made against Joseph Smith. In repentant humility, the Pratts sought readmission to the Church, and both were rebaptized by the Prophet Joseph on

January 20, 1843. Elder Pratt was restored to his apostolic office and, like Elder Hyde before him, took his original seat of seniority, where he remained until June of 1875, when John Taylor was rightfully placed ahead of him in seniority.

Some years later, Elder Taylor discussed his feelings about the matter of seniority involving Elders Hyde and Pratt:

> Orson Hyde and Orson Pratt had both of them been disfellowshipped and dropped from their quorum, and when they returned, without any particular investigation or arrangement, they took the position in the quorum which they had formerly occupied, and as there was no objection raised, or investigation had on this subject, things continued in this position for a number of years. Some ten or twelve years ago, Brother George A. Smith drew my attention to this matter. I think it was soon after he was appointed as counselor to the first presidency; and he asked me if I had noticed the impropriety of the arrangement. He stated that these brethren having been dropped from the quorum could not assume the position that they before had in the quorum; but that all those who remained in the quorum when they had left it must necessarily take the precedence of them in the quorum. He stated, at the same time, that these questions might become very serious ones, in case of change of circumstances arising from death or otherwise; remarking also, that I stood before them in the quorum. I told him I was aware of that, and of the correctness of the position assumed by him, and had been for years, but that I did not choose to agitate or bring up a question of that kind. Furthermore, I stated that, personally, I cared nothing about the matter, and, moreover, I entertained a very high esteem for both the parties named; while, at the same time, I could not help but see, with him, that complications might hereafter arise, unless the matter were adjusted. Some time after, in Sanpete, in

June, 1875, President Young brought up the subject of seniority, and stated that John Taylor was the man that stood next to him; and that where he was not, John Taylor presided. He also made the statement that Brother Hyde and Brother Pratt were not in their right positions in the quorum. (*Gospel Kingdom,* sel. G. Homer Durham [Salt Lake City: Bookcraft, 1964], pp. 191–92.)

In this manner an important development in the principles governing succession had been established. The "Senior Apostle [is the one] holding the oldest ordination without interruption." (*Journal of Discourses,* 19:234.) Continuous service in the Quorum of the Twelve was just as essential as the date of one's ordination. Elders Hyde and Pratt lost their seniority as a result of an interruption in their service in that quorum.

John Taylor presided over the Church as the President of the Quorum of the Twelve Apostles from the death of Brigham Young until October 10, 1880, when the First Presidency was reorganized. Elder Taylor was sustained as the President of the Church with two fellow quorum members, George Q. Cannon and Joseph F. Smith, as his counselors.

Why was there a three-year interim between the death of Brigham Young and the reorganization of the First Presidency? At the time the Twelve were sustained to lead the Church, on October 8, 1877, Elder George Q. Cannon explained:

> Well . . . says one, Why cannot you organize a First Presidency now, if the Twelve have this authority? Do you want to know the reason, brethren and sisters, why we do not take such a step? I suspect you would like to know why a man and his two Counselors are not singled out, called and set apart by the voice of the people at this Conference, as the First Presidency of the Church?

The reason is simply this: the Lord has not revealed it to us; he has not commanded us to do this, and until he does require this at our hands, we shall not do it. . . . When the voice of God comes, when it shall be the counsel of our Heavenly Father that a First Presidency shall be again organized, the Quorum of the Twelve will be organized in its fullness as before. Therefore you can wait, as well as we, for the voice of the Lord. (*Journal of Discourses,* 19:236–37.)

That unmistakable voice came some three years later, and on October 10, 1880, the First Presidency was reorganized.

Wilford Woodruff as Senior Apostle

On July 25, 1887, the spirit of President John Taylor left his earthly tabernacle to begin his labors on the other side of the veil that separates mortals from those of the unseen world of spirits and resurrected beings. The mantle of the presiding officer of the Church was passed to the next senior apostle, Wilford Woodruff. As previously explained, Elder Woodruff was ordained as one of the Twelve on April 26, 1839, and was widely known for his faithful service in his sacred office.

At the October conference of 1887, continuing the pattern followed at the deaths of Joseph Smith and Brigham Young, the Quorum of the Twelve Apostles was sustained as the governing council of the Church, with Wilford Woodruff as President. In expressing himself about his position as the presiding officer of the Church, President Woodruff said: "President John Taylor's death places the chief responsibility and care of the Church of Latter-day Saints upon my shoulders, in connection with the Twelve, which now become the presiding authority of the Church. . . . It is a position I have never looked for, but in the providence of God this new responsibility is thrown upon me. . . . I never expected to outlive President Taylor, but God has ordained otherwise." (In Matthias F. Cowley, *Wilford Woodruff* [Salt Lake City: Bookcraft, 1964], p. 560.)

On April 7, 1889, the First Presidency was again established as a separate quorum of three presiding high priests, with Wilford Woodruff as President and George Q. Cannon and Joseph F. Smith as his counselors. This presidency served until President Woodruff's death on September 2, 1898.

Lorenzo Snow as the Senior Apostle

Lorenzo Snow was eighty-four years of age when he became the senior apostle of the Church and kingdom of God on earth. The day following the funeral of President Woodruff, the Twelve met in council in the the Salt Lake Temple. In great humility, recognizing the limitations of his age, Lorenzo Snow offered to vacate his position as the senior apostle in deference to any others of the quorum whom the members of the council might choose to be their leader. The response of the Twelve was to immediately sustain him as their rightful leader—as President of the Twelve.

Several days later, on September 13, the members of the Quorum of the Twelve sustained Lorenzo Snow as the President of the Church, with George Q. Cannon and Joseph F. Smith as his counselors in the First Presidency. This was the first time there had not been a long delay between the death of the previous prophet and the reorganization of the First Presidency.

There are several reasons why this occurred. First, almost six years before his death, Wilford Woodruff had instructed Lorenzo Snow on this matter. He said, "It was not the will of the Lord that in the future there should be a lengthy period elapse between the death of the president and the re-organization of the First Presidency." (Smith, *Essentials in Church History,* p. 501; see also *Elders Journal* 4:110–11.)

Most importantly, Lorenzo Snow had been instructed by the Savior himself on this matter. President Snow had earnestly prayed in the Salt Lake Temple for the life of Wilford Woodruff to be extended beyond his own. "Nevertheless," the humble man petitioned, "Thy will be done. I have not sought this responsibility but if it be Thy will, I now present myself before Thee for Thy guidance and instruction." His prayerful pleadings were answered by a personal visit from the resurrected Lord, who instructed him regarding the reorganization of the presidency. (Thomas C. Romney, *The Life of Lorenzo Snow* [Salt Lake City: Deseret Book, 1955], p. 445.)

Joseph F. Smith as Senior Apostle

Joseph F. Smith's rise to the position of senior apostle had an interesting history. Following a meeting of the First Presidency and Quorum of the Twelve on July 1, 1866, Brigham Young announced to the Brethren that he felt impressed by the Spirit to ordain the twenty-seven-year-old son of the martyred Patriarch Hyrum Smith as an apostle and to call him as an additional counselor to the First Presidency.

At the time of his call, there was no vacancy in the Quorum of the Twelve. Not until October 8, 1867, was Joseph F. Smith set apart as a member of the Quorum of the Twelve Apostles, filling the vacancy created by the dropping of Amasa Lyman from the quorum.

One year later, Brigham Young, Jr., was called to fill a vacancy in the Quorum of the Twelve created by the call of Apostle George A. Smith to serve in the First Presidency in the place of Heber C. Kimball, who had passed away the previous summer. The thirty-year-old son of the President of the Church had been ordained an apostle by his father four years earlier on February 4, 1864.

At the October conference in 1868, Brigham Young, Jr.,

was sustained as the junior member of the Quorum of the Twelve, right behind Joseph F. Smith. However, at the following conference in April of 1869, his name was placed ahead of Joseph F. Smith's. This probably was done on the basis of the earlier ordination as an apostle that Brigham, Jr., had received. This order of apostolic seniority prevailed until 1900, although during much of this time seniority was not an issue because Joseph F. Smith was serving as a counselor in the First Presidency.

At a meeting of the First Presidency held on March 31, 1900, President Lorenzo Snow noted that since the death of Elder Franklin D. Richards the previous December, the apostle who was next to him in seniority was his first counselor, George Q. Cannon. He told President Cannon that he could step down from the First Presidency to preside over the Twelve if he desired to do so, but his counselor declined. President Snow also noted that Joseph F. Smith should be senior to Brigham Young, Jr., and this matter was brought up in a meeting of the First Presidency and Quorum of the Twelve on April 5, 1900.

Joseph F. Smith described the important decision regarding apostolic seniority that was reached on that occasion:

> It was unanimously decided that the acceptance of a member into the council or quorum of the Twelve fixed his rank or position in the Apostleship. That *the Apostles took precedence from the date they entered the quorum.* Thus today, President Snow is the senior Apostle. President George Q. Cannon next, myself next, Brigham Young [Jr.] next, Francis M. Lyman next, and so on to the last one received into the quorum. In the case of the death of President Snow, President Cannon surviving him, would succeed to the Presidency, and so on according to seniority in the Apostleship of the Twelve; that ordination to the Apostleship under the

hands of any Apostle other than to fill a vacancy in the quorum, and authorized by the General Authorities of the Church did not count in precedence; that if the First Presidency were dissolved by the death of the President, his counselors having been ordained Apostles in the Quorum of the Twelve would resume their places in the quorum, according to the seniority of their ordinations into that quorum. This important ruling settles a long unsettled point, and is most timely. (In Joseph Fielding Smith, *The Life of Joseph F. Smith* [Salt Lake City: Deseret Book, 1969], pp. 310–11; italics added.)

The timeliness of this decision is reflected in the fact that President Cannon passed away one year and one week after this decision had been reached (April 12, 1901), which placed Joseph F. Smith as the next senior apostle to the President of the Church. On October 6, 1901, Joseph F. Smith was sustained as the first counselor in the First Presidency, with Rudger Clawson as second counselor to President Snow. Four days later, Lorenzo Snow died, and Joseph F. Smith became the senior apostle, one position ahead of Brigham Young, Jr.

On October 17, 1901, one week after the death of President Snow, Joseph F. Smith was sustained as the sixth President of The Church of Jesus Christ of Latter-day Saints. He was the first one to come to this position after having served as a counselor in the First Presidency, but, as was the case with each of his predecessors, he was the recognized senior apostle on earth.

Note also the circumstances of Joseph F. Smith's being set apart to his presiding position as President of the Church. The patriarch of the Church, John Smith, was invited by President Smith to stand in the circle with the members of the Twelve Apostles and be mouth in pronouncing the blessing given to Joseph F. Smith on that special occasion. While the patriarch did not hold the apostolic keys, one must understand that this setting apart was not a conferral of keys; for, as previously pointed out, President Joseph F. Smith already possessed the keys of the priesthood in their fulness by virtue of his apostolic office. This setting apart was simply the conferral of a *priesthood blessing,* which the patriarch, by virtue of his holding the Melchizedek Priesthood and having been invited by the senior apostle to do so, had a right to bestow.

One other interesting aspect of the reorganization of the First Presidency under President Smith was his choice of counselors. Since the days of Brigham Young, the President's counselors had held the apostolic office (although several of President Young's counselors were ordained as apostles but not set apart as members of the Quorum of the Twelve.)

Joseph F. Smith reached beyond the Quorum of the Twelve in selecting his first counselor: John R. Winder, the second counselor in the presiding bishopric, was chosen to serve as first counselor in the First Presidency. President Smith did not follow the pattern of Brigham Young in conferring the apostolic office upon President Winder. One is reminded that the only office specified by the scriptures as being a requisite for serving in the First Presidency is that of high priest. (See D&C 107:22.) President Smith did take his other counselor from the Quorum of the Twelve: fellow apostle Anthon H. Lund was selected as the second counselor in the First Presidency.

President Joseph F. Smith presided over the Church as the senior apostle until his death on November 19, 1918.

Heber J. Grant as Senior Apostle

Heber J. Grant was ordained an apostle on October 16, 1882, when he was only twenty-five years of age. Thirty-four years later, on November 23, 1916, he was sustained as President of the Quorum of the Twelve Apostles following the death of the man who stood ahead of him in seniority, President Francis M. Lyman.

Heber J. Grant served as President of the Twelve for almost two years before the passing of President Joseph F. Smith. President Grant related the following regarding his last conversation with his predecessor. "The last words uttered by President Joseph F. Smith were to the effect, when he shook hands with me — he died that night — 'The Lord bless you, my boy, the Lord bless you; you have got a great responsibility. Always remember this is the Lord's work and not man's. The Lord is greater than any man. He knows whom He wants to lead His Church, and never makes any mistakes. The Lord bless you.' " ("President Grant's Opening Conference Message," *Improvement Era,* May 1941, p. 267.)

Four days after the death of President Smith, Heber J. Grant was sustained as the President of the Church, with Anthon H. Lund as his first counselor in the First Presidency and Charles W. Penrose as second counselor. Both of these men held the apostolic office and had served in the previous First Presidency under President Joseph F. Smith.

President Grant's first experience in filling a vacancy in the Quorum of the Twelve was a spiritual highlight that convinced him that the Lord was the one who ultimately selected those who would hold the apostolic office. For almost two months following his being sustained as President of the Church, Heber J. Grant prayed and pondered about who should fill the vacancy that existed in the Twelve. His mind continuously reflected on the name of Richard W. Young, who was not only a dear friend of President Grant, but who seemed eminently qualified by talent, experience, and spiritual depth to serve as one of the Lord's special witnesses. Richard Young was a retired general of the army, a lawyer, a successful businessman, a stake president, and the grandson of the late Brigham Young.

On January 7, 1919, after conferring with his counselors, President Grant wrote the name of Richard W. Young on a slip of paper, which he put in his pocket as he prepared to go to the temple to meet with the First Presidency and the members of the Quorum of the Twelve Apostles. At the appointed time in the meeting, he reached in his pocket and retrieved the piece of paper with his friend's name on it. However, rather than presenting the name of Richard W. Young as the one to fill the vacancy among the Twelve, he presented the name of a man he hardly knew: Melvin J. Ballard. At the time Elder Ballard was serving as president of the Northwestern States Mission. (See Francis M. Gibbons, *Heber J. Grant* [Salt Lake City: Deseret Book, 1979], p. 175.)

Years later, as he reflected on that singular experience, President Grant testified: "I have felt the inspiration of the Living God directing me in my labors. From the day that I chose a comparative stranger to be one of the Apostles, instead of my lifelong and dearest living friend, I have known as I know that I live, that I am entitled to the light and the inspiration and the guidance of God in directing His work here upon this earth; and I know, as I know that I live, that it is God's work, and that Jesus Christ is the Son of the Living God, the Redeemer of the world." (In Conference Report, April 1941, p. 6.)

One significant development regarding the presiding officer over the Quorum of the Twelve occurred during Heber J. Grant's administration. Because Anthon H. Lund, who was second in apostolic seniority to President Grant, was serving in the First Presidency, Rudger Clawson, third in apostolic seniority, was sustained as "Acting President" of the Quorum of the Twelve in June 1919. In April 1920, in addition to being sustained as first counselor in the First Presidency, President Lund was also sustained as President of the Quorum of the Twelve, with Rudger Clawson as Acting President.

This action affirmed President Grant's belief that the apostle who stood next in seniority to the President of the Church should be called the "President of the Twelve," even though other duties may preclude his actually administering the affairs of the Quorum of the Twelve.

Several interesting moves involving seniority and position in the Twelve occurred during President Grant's administration. The first one involved J. Reuben Clark, Jr., the U.S. ambassador to Mexico, who was called to serve as second counselor in the First Presidency on April 6, 1933. President Clark had not been a member of the Quorum of the Twelve. Following the death of Anthony W. Ivins, first counselor in the First Presidency, President Clark was called to serve as first counselor, with David O. McKay as second counselor. They were sustained to their positions in October 1934. However, the name of J. Reuben Clark, Jr., was also presented as a member of the Quorum of the Twelve Apostles along with Alonzo A. Hinckley, making a total of thirteen names presented from that quorum. Although he served in the First Presidency until his death in 1961, this move established J. Reuben Clark's seniority among the ordained apostles in the First Presidency and Quorum of the Twelve.

The other interesting move regarding the apostolic office involved Sylvester Q. Cannon, who served as Presiding Bishop of the Church from 1925 until 1938. He was released from the bishopric at the April conference in 1938 and sustained as an "Associate to the Quorum of the Twelve Apostles." Elder Cannon was ordained to the apostolic office on April 14, 1938. He was sustained as a member of the Quorum of the Twelve on October 6, 1939, following the death of Elder Melvin J. Ballard.

George Albert Smith as Senior Apostle

President Heber J. Grant passed away on May 14, 1945, and one week later George Albert Smith was sustained as the President of the Church. President Smith had served as President of the Quorum of the Twelve and been the next senior apostle to President Grant since July 1, 1943.

George Albert Smith was ordained an apostle on October 8, 1903, at the age of thirty-three. Because of ill health, he was unable to serve actively in the Quorum of the Twelve from 1909 to 1912. However, during this time he continued to be sustained as a member of that governing body. Thus, there was no interruption in his service that might have affected his seniority among the apostles.

President Smith invited the two counselors who had served his predecessor—J. Reuben Clark, Jr., and David O. McKay—to continue to serve with him in his presidency. He led the Church as President and senior apostle until he passed away on April 4, 1951.

David O. McKay as Senior Apostle

In August of 1950, the man who stood next to George Albert Smith in seniority—President George F. Richards—passed away. At the October general conference of the Church, David O. McKay, who now stood next to President Smith in seniority, was sustained not only as the second counselor in the First Presidency, but also as the President of the Quorum of the Twelve Apostles. The next apostle in seniority, Joseph Fielding Smith, was sustained as the Acting President of the Twelve.

Five days after the death of George Albert Smith, David O. McKay was sustained as the President of the Church. In a surprising move, President McKay selected the third senior apostle, Stephen L Richards, as his first counselor and J. Reuben Clark, Jr., as his second counselor. President Clark had served the two previous Presidents as their first counselor, and many were puzzled by President McKay's actions.

President McKay explained:

I thoughtfully and prayerfully considered what two men would be most helpful and most contributive to the advancement of the Church. The impression came, I am sure, directly from Him whose Church this is, and who presides over it, that the two counselors whom you have this day approved should be the other members of the quorum of the First Presidency. Both are members of the Council of the Twelve, though counselors might have been chosen from High Priests outside the presiding body.

I chose these two members from the Council of the Twelve — two men with whom I have labored closely for many years, whose worth, whose ability I know. I have been associated with Elder Richards directly in Church affairs and in presiding positions for over thirty years. I have been associated with President Clark in two quorums of the First Presidency for over sixteen years. With these and other facts in mind, the question arose as to the order they should occupy in this new quorum.

Each man I love. Each man is capable in his particular lines, and particularly with respect to the welfare and advancement of the Kingdom of God.

I realized that there would be a question in the minds of some as to which one of the two should be chosen as first counselor. That question resolved itself in my mind first as to the order of precedence, seniority in the Council of the Twelve Apostles. That should make no difference according to the practice of the Church, because members of the Council had heretofore been chosen irrespective of the position a member occupied in the Council of the Twelve. And, as I have already said, high Priests have been chosen even as first counselors who were not members of the Council.

I felt that one guiding principle in this choice would be to follow the seniority in the Council. These two men were sitting in their places in that presiding body in the Church, and I felt impressed that it would be advisable to continue that same seniority in the new quorum of the First Presidency. I repeat, *not as an established policy,* but because it seemed advisable in view of my close relationship to these two choice leaders. (In Conference Report, Apr. 1951, pp. 150–51; italics added.)

President Stephen L Richards passed away on May 19, 1959, and President Clark was once again sustained as first counselor in the First Presidency, with Henry D. Moyle of the Council of the Twelve as second counselor. Two years later, on June 22, 1961, because of the failing health of President Clark, an additional counselor was called to serve in the First Presidency: Hugh B. Brown was called from the Twelve to fill this position, and he was replaced in the Quorum of the Twelve by Gordon B. Hinckley. It is ironic that twenty years later Elder Hinckley himself would be called from among the Twelve to serve as an additional counselor in the presidency of President Spencer W. Kimball.

When President Clark passed away, Henry D. Moyle and Hugh B. Brown were sustained as first and second counselors respectively in the First Presidency. Following the death of President Moyle, Hugh B. Brown became first counselor, and the junior member of the Quorum of the Twelve, Nathan Eldon Tanner, was called as second counselor.

In October of 1965, President McKay called President Joseph Fielding Smith of the Twelve, and Elder Thorpe B. Isaacson, an Assistant to the Twelve, as additional counselors in the First Presidency. President Smith retained his position as President of the Twelve and served in a dual capacity. Two years later, another Assistant to the Twelve, Elder Alvin R. Dyer, was ordained an apostle but not given membership in the Quorum of the Twelve, which had no vacancy. In April of 1968, Elder Dyer was sustained as another counselor in the First Presidency, bringing the total in that presiding body to six.

Following the death of President McKay on January 18, 1970, both Elders Isaacson and Dyer were sustained once again as Assistants to the Twelve. Elder Dyer, who lived until March 6, 1977, never did receive membership in the Quorum of the Twelve even though he had been ordained an apostle. He died as a member of the First Quorum of the Seventy, to which office he had been sustained in October of 1976.

As on previous occasions, those counselors in the First Presidency who had been ordained apostles and been previously sustained as members of the Quorum of the Twelve Apostles resumed their positions in this governing body. Thus, for the moment at least, the Quorum had fourteen members. (See Spencer W. Kimball, "The Need for a Prophet," *Improvement Era,* June 1970, p. 92.)

Joseph Fielding Smith as Senior Apostle

Joseph Fielding Smith was ordained as an apostle on April 7, 1910, and was in his sixtieth year of service in that quorum at the time he became President of the Church. He had been sustained as the President of the Quorum of the Twelve on April 9, 1951, and stood second in apostolic seniority to David O. McKay for nineteen years. He was sustained as President of the Church on January 23, 1970.

President Smith chose the next senior apostle, Harold B. Lee, as his first counselor in the newly reorganized First Presidency. President Lee was also sustained as the President of the Quorum of the Twelve, and the third-ranking apostle, Spencer W. Kimball, was chosen as the Acting President of the Twelve. Nathan Eldon Tanner, who had served as second counselor to President McKay, was asked to continue as second counselor to President Smith. Hugh B. Brown returned to service in the Quorum of the Twelve.

Joseph Fielding Smith, at the age of 93, is the oldest man to have become the senior apostle on earth. Prior to his call as President of the Church, he had served longer than any other man in the Quorum of the Twelve Apostles and is only exceeded in combined service in the Quorum of the Twelve and the First Presidency by Presidents David O. McKay and Heber J. Grant. President Smith died on July 2, 1972, less than three weeks short of his ninety-sixth birthday.

Harold B. Lee as Senior Apostle

On July 7, 1972, the fourteen men who held the apostolic office and who had been sustained as members of the Quorum of the Twelve met in solemn council to consider the reorganization of the presidency. Their quorum president, Harold B. Lee, presided and conducted the meeting.

One of those present, N. Eldon Tanner, reported on the proceedings: "At this meeting we called upon the Lord in solemn prayer. Then each member of the Twelve, starting with the junior member, was called by the President of the Quorum to express his feelings regarding the matter at hand. When it became President Kimball's turn to speak, he, at the conclusion of his remarks, nominated President Harold B. Lee as President of the Church, which motion was duly seconded and put to the Twelve and carried unanimously." ("The Priesthood and Its Presidency," *Ensign,* Jan. 1973, p. 100.)

Thus, Harold B. Lee became the eleventh President of The Church of Jesus Christ of Latter-day Saints. He had been ordained an apostle thirty-one years earlier, on April 10, 1941. It is of interest to note that in selecting his counselors, he chose the junior of the two to serve as his first counselor, thus departing from the pattern used by David O. McKay at the time he selected his first and second counselors.

President Lee asked Nathan Eldon Tanner, who had

served with him in the First Presidency under Joseph Fielding Smith, to serve as his first counselor. Marion G. Romney, who was third in apostolic seniority (behind President Lee and Spencer W. Kimball) was invited to serve as the second counselor in the new presidency.

Spencer W. Kimball as Senior Apostle

President Harold B. Lee passed away unexpectedly on December 26, 1973. At the time of his passing, his second counselor, Marion G. Romney, and the President of the Twelve, Spencer W. Kimball, were both in the hospital where President Lee was being cared for. During the anxious moments when the medical personnel frantically worked on preserving the life of the unconscious leader of the Church, President Kimball paid deference to President Romney, the presiding officer of the Church on the scene. However, as soon as it was determined that life had passed from their beloved prophet, the transition of authority immediately took place, and Marion G. Romney was asking his new file leader, President Spencer W. Kimball, what he wanted him to do.

Elder Bruce R. McConkie described the significance of this occasion:

> At the moment [President Lee] passed, Brother Romney, in harmony with the system and the established tradition and custom of the Church, stepped aside, and President Spencer W. Kimball was then in complete charge and had total direction. President Kimball was at that moment the senior apostle of God on earth. And as the last heartbeat of President Lee ceased, the mantle of leadership passed to President Kimball, whose next heartbeat was that of the living oracle and presiding authority of God on earth. From that moment, the Church continued under the direction of President Kimball. ("Succession in the Presidency," in *BYU Speeches*

of the Year 1974 [Provo: Brigham Young University Press, 1975], p. 19.)

Commenting on the place of direct revelation in this transition of authority, Elder McConkie further stated: "It was not required, nor was it requisite or needed, that the Lord give any revelation, that any special direction be given. The law was already ordained and established. . . . And so it was with the transfer of leadership from President Lee to President Kimball."

On December 30, 1973, fourteen apostles convened for a sacred and solemn meeting in the Salt Lake Temple under the direction of the senior member of that body, Spencer W. Kimball. The two counselors who had served President Lee both held the apostolic office and had been members of the Quorum of the Twelve prior to their call to serve in the First Presidency. They took their regular places among the other apostles according to their order of seniority. Spencer W. Kimball and Ezra Taft Benson had both been ordained as apostles on October 7, 1943, but President Kimball was the senior apostle of the two because he had been ordained and set apart as a member of the Quorum before Elder Benson.

Following some remarks by President Kimball, each member of the quorum, starting with Ezra Taft Benson and continuing to the junior member of the group, was invited to express himself on the issue of reorganizing the First Presidency. There was no question about who should be the presiding officer. The Brethren were unanimous in their desire to proceed according to the divinely established pattern. Spencer W. Kimball was "chosen by the body" (D&C 107:22) to be the President of the Church and to be sustained as the prophet, seer, and revelator to the Church as well as its Trustee-in-Trust.

He retained the two counselors who had served President Lee — N. Eldon Tanner and Marion G. Romney. Elder Gordon B. Hinckley was called as an additional counselor in the First Presidency on July 23, 1981. The call was providential, for within a few months President Kimball's failing health put an added responsibility upon the counselors. President Tanner passed away in November of 1982, and Marion G. Romney was sustained as first counselor with Gordon B. Hinckley as second counselor.

The strength of a strong counselor was evidenced as time passed and age took its terrible toll on the health of Presidents Kimball and Romney. President Hinckley had to shoulder what he later referred to as "an almost overwhelming burden of responsibility" for the day-to-day duties of the First Presidency. Reflecting on these times, he said: "I counseled frequently with my Brethren of the Twelve, and I cannot say enough of appreciation to them for their understanding and for the wisdom of their judgment. In matters where there was a well-established policy, we moved forward. But no new policy was announced or implemented, and no significant practice was altered without sitting down with President Kimball and laying the matter before him and receiving his full consent and full approval." ("In Counsellors There Is Safety," *Ensign,* Nov. 1990, p. 50.)

In the Lord's perfect system of governing the affairs of His kingdom, He had made provision for the continuous and consistent guidance of His church by His chosen servants. In the event of an incapacitating illness, or the inaccessibility of the presiding officer of the Church or quorum, the next senior man may take charge.

President Hinckley provided this explanation:

> Some people, most of them not members of the Church, worry because the President of the Church is an elderly man. I want to assure you that under the organization put in place by the Lord himself, there is no need to worry. The President has two counselors. So

long as either of them is able to function, there will be an active First Presidency with full powers of decision in all matters affecting the Church. [See D&C 90:6.]

Associated with the Presidency is the Council of the Twelve Apostles. At times in the history of the Church, when there was no First Presidency, the Council of the Twelve governed its affairs. As a matter of fact, these were some of the most difficult and demanding times in the history of the Church. . . .

The Lord will not allow his work to suffer. He will not allow it to be led astray. He has made that clear. There is much of flexibility and resiliency in this inspired organization. It can accommodate almost any imaginable set of circumstances. ("The Sustaining of Church Officers," *Ensign,* Nov. 1984, pp. 4–5.)

Ezra Taft Benson as Senior Apostle

President Kimball passed away on November 5, 1985, and, as will always be the case upon the death of the prophet, the First Presidency was dissolved, and the leadership of the Church devolved upon the Quorum of the Twelve Apostles. The two former counselors to President Kimball took their places of seniority among the fourteen apostles who constituted the quorum. The senior apostle of this body was Ezra Taft Benson.

President Benson had been an apostle since October 7, 1943, and had continuously been sustained as a member of that governing body since his ordination. With the approval of President David O. McKay, there was an eight-year period from 1953 to 1961 when Elder Benson had limited service in the Twelve because of his service as the Secretary of Agriculture in the cabinet of U.S. President Dwight D. Eisenhower. However, he was not dropped from the quorum during this period, and therefore his standing in seniority in the council was not impacted.

Thus, at a solemn meeting in the Salt Lake Temple on November 10, 1985, there was no question in the minds of the apostles that Ezra Taft Benson was their leader. He was unanimously sustained by his fellow apostles as the President of the Church, with all of the rights and authority accompanying that high and holy calling. President Benson selected two of his fellow apostles, Gordon B. Hinckley and Thomas S. Monson, to serve as his first and second counselors respectively.

Marion G. Romney was second in seniority to President Benson and was sustained as the President of the Quorum of the Twelve. Because of President Romney's failing health, the man who stood next to President Romney in apostolic seniority, Howard W. Hunter, was named as the Acting President of the Twelve. Once again the Lord's perfect system worked without a hitch and without any uncertainty on the part of those men who understand the apostolic order of succession.

Though vigorous in the first years of his administration, President Benson also began to feel the limitations imposed by age. As always, strong counselors, acting in behalf of the prophet, shouldered more of the burden of governing the affairs of the Church. Once again, President Gordon B. Hinckley spoke of the carefulness with which he and his associate in the First Presidency moved forward:

> President Benson . . . does not have the strength or vitality he once possessed in abundance. Brother [Thomas S.] Monson and I, as his counselors, do as has been done before, and that is to move forward the work of the Church, while being very careful not to get ahead of the President nor to undertake any departure of any kind from long-established policy without his knowledge and full approval. . . . We postpone action when we are not fully certain of our course and do not move forward

until we have the blessing of our President and that assurance which comes from the Spirit of the Lord. ("In Counsellors There Is Safety," pp. 50–51.)

The Lord Is in Charge

Some have wondered why the Lord has allowed prophets to suffer physical limitations that restrict their ability to serve as they would like to. Elder Boyd K. Packer gave some insights regarding the aging process that imposes limitations upon the Lord's leaders: "There are councils and counselors and quorums to counterbalance the foibles and frailties of man. The Lord organized His church to provide for mortal men to work as mortal men, and yet He assured that the spirit of revelation would guide in all that we do in His name." ("Revelation in a Changing World," *Ensign,* Nov. 1989, p. 16.) Thus, while we do not know the reasons why prophets and other leaders are allowed to linger in ill health, this much we know: the Lord is in charge!

Suffice it to say that the Lord is all-wise and all-knowing. His ways are proper, and there is divine purpose in all He does. It is well to ponder these inspired words of holy writ: "For my thoughts are not your thoughts, neither are your ways my ways, saith the Lord. For as the heavens are higher than the earth, so are my ways higher than your ways, and my thoughts than your thoughts." (Isa. 55:8–9.)

The Lord reminded the Prophet Joseph Smith that "the works, and the designs, and the purposes of God cannot be frustrated, neither can they come to naught." (D&C 3:1.) God is in charge. He selects His servants. He knows whom He wants to preside in His church. He places the apostles in their callings at the appropriate time in His divine plan. He will release them when His purposes are fulfilled.

President Gordon B. Hinckley explained that as long as the current prophet was living, regardless of the limitations that health imposed upon him, he would be the presiding officer of the Church. "None other can or will take his place for so long as he lives. When he passes, there will be another ready, a man who, through long years of experience and service, has been trained, has been tested, has been schooled and refined and prepared to fill that sacred and awesome responsibility." ("The Cornerstones of Our Faith," *Ensign,* Nov. 1984, p. 50.)

That man will have served his apprenticeship as a member of the Quorum of the Twelve Apostles and will, step-by-step, have climbed the ladder of seniority according to the will of the Lord. President Spencer W. Kimball provided this insightful summary on the procedure of succession: "Since the death of his servants is in the power and control of the Lord, he permits to come to the first place only the one who is destined to take that leadership. Death and life become the controlling factors. Each new apostle in turn is chosen by the Lord and revealed to the then living prophet who ordains him. The matter of seniority is basic in the first quorum of the Church. All the apostles understand this perfectly, and all well-trained members of the Church are conversant with this perfect succession program." ("We Thank Thee, O God, for a Prophet," *Ensign,* Jan. 1973, p. 34.)

Chapter Six

The Senior Apostle and Apostolic Succession

The Nature of the Apostolic Keys

The far-reaching nature of the apostolic keys was described by Brigham Young: "The keys of the eternal Priesthood, which is after the order of the Son of God, is comprehended by being an Apostle. All the Priesthood, all the keys, all the gifts, all the endowments, and everything preparatory to entering back into the presence of the Father and of the Son, is in, composed of, circumscribed by, or I might say incorporated within the circumference of the Apostleship." (*Millennial Star* 15:489.)

In order for one to lead the Church, it is not sufficient for that person to have received the priesthood or have been ordained to an office therein. The rightful leaders of the Lord's church and kingdom on earth also must have received the keys of presidency. Those keys are vested in the apostolic office of the men who have been properly ordained as apostles and been given membership in the Quorum of the Twelve Apostles.

"These keys are the right of presidency," said President Joseph Fielding Smith. "They are the power and authority to govern and direct all of the Lord's affairs on earth. Those who hold them have power to govern and control the manner in which all others may serve in the priesthood. [Those who] hold the priesthood ... can only use it as authorized and directed so to do by those who hold the keys." ("Eternal Keys and the Right to Preside," *Ensign,* July 1972, p. 87.)

Inherent within one's ordination to the apostolic office is the right to function within any office in the Church. This includes the authority to serve as the presiding officer in the First Presidency — the President of the Church — if the one ordained becomes the senior apostle.

President Harold B. Lee observed:

The beginning of the call of one to be President of the Church actually begins when he is called, ordained, and set apart to become a member of the Quorum of the Twelve Apostles. Such a call by prophecy, or in other words, by the inspiration of the Lord to the one holding the keys of presidency, and the subsequent ordination and setting apart by the laying on of hands by that same authority, places each apostle in a priesthood quorum of twelve men holding the apostleship.

Each apostle so ordained under the hands of the President of the Church, who holds the keys of the kingdom of God in concert with all other ordained apostles, has given to him the priesthood authority necessary to hold every position in the Church, even to a position of presidency over the Church if he were called by the presiding authority and sustained by a vote of a constituent assembly of the membership of the Church. ("The Day in Which We Live," p. 28.)

In this respect, note the comments of Elder George Q. Cannon regarding Brigham Young's selection of Elder

107

George A. Smith to serve as a counselor in the First Presidency of the Church:

> President Young, when he chose brother George A. Smith to be his First Counselor, in the place of Heber C. Kimball, did not lay his hands upon his head to confer upon him any additional power or authority for the position, because brother George A. held the Apostleship in its fulness, and by virtue of that Priesthood he could act in that or in any other position in the Church. He chose other assistant Counselors; he did not set them apart, there was no necessity for it, as they already held the Apostleship. And if he had, he could only have blessed them; he could not bestow upon them any more than they already had, because they had all that he himself had, that is when he chose them from the same Quorum. (*Journal of Discourses,* 19:235.)

Elder Cannon went on to say that no man who has been ordained to the apostolic office needs to have hands laid on his head and be given any additional authority when called to serve in the presidency of the Church because such a man "already possesse[s] the power, authority and ordination." He noted that such settings apart would not be wrong or improper, but they must be seen as the conferring of a blessing rather than the bestowal of any authority. Such blessings "would not bestow upon him any additional authority or any more keys, presuming that he already had received the fulness of the Apostleship." (*Journal of Discourses,* 19:236.)

The Apostolic Office Is Conferred by Those in Authority

The apostles hold their keys by virtue of having been called of God and having been properly ordained by those who are recognized by the Church as having the apostolic authority. Ordination to this holy office is not done clandestinely. It follows the order set forth by the Lord in the scriptures: "It shall not be given to any one to go forth to preach my gospel, or to build up my church, except he be ordained by some one who has authority, and it is known to the church that he has authority and has been regularly ordained by the heads of the church." (D&C 42:11.) Furthermore, the Prophet Joseph Smith declared as one of our fundamental statements of belief: "We believe that a man must be called of God, by prophecy, and by the laying on of hands by those who are in authority, to preach the Gospel and administer in the ordinances thereof." (A of F 1:5.)

The apostolic office is conferred upon one "called of God" by those who themselves have received that holy office from "those who are in authority," having "been regularly ordained by the heads of the church." These men can trace their keys of priesthood authority in an unbroken chain back to the Twelve of Joseph Smith's day, and through him to the heavenly messengers sent from the presence of the Lord Himself to bestow those keys.

The Apostles Must Be Sustained in Their Callings

In addition to their having been ordained as apostles and set apart as members of the Quorum of the Twelve, each of these men has also been sustained to his calling by a constituent body of the Church. Elder John A. Widtsoe explained the necessity of common consent by those who are to be governed:

> Every officer of the Priesthood or auxiliary organizations, though properly nominated, holds his position in the Church only with the consent of the people. Officers may be nominated by the Presidency of the Church, but unless the people accept them as officials, they cannot exercise the authority of the offices to which they have been called. All things in the Church must be done by common consent. This makes the people, men

and women, under God, the rulers of the Church. Even the President of the Church, before he can fully enter upon his duties, or continue in the office, must be sustained by the people. (*Priesthood and Church Government*, pp. 233–34.)

The Doctrine and Covenants underscores the relationship between one's being called of God and then sustained or upheld by the people: "The president of the church . . . is *appointed* by revelation, and *acknowledged* in his administration by the voice of the church." (D&C 102:9; italics added.) The Lord declared: "No person is to be ordained to any office in this church, where there is a regularly organized branch of the same, without the vote of that church." (D&C 20:65.)

Thus the members of the Church participate in a theocratic form of government. God makes the selection of His servants, they are called and set apart by duly recognized leaders of the Church, but they must also be approved and sustained by those they are called to govern, or, perhaps better said, called to serve.

The principle of common consent must not be misunderstood. Although the Lord has given His people the option of voting to "approve" or to "disapprove" the names of those placed before them (D&C 124:144), one must not capriciously, without proper cause, vote against a duly appointed officer of the Church. The Lord declared that the process of common consent in the Church should be accompanied "by much prayer and faith." (D&C 26:2.) This presupposes that Church members will be in tune with the Spirit when they participate in the sustaining process.

While serving as a member of the Quorum of the Twelve, President Joseph Fielding Smith cautioned that

no man has the right to raise his hand in opposition, or with contrary vote, unless he has a reason for doing so that would be valid if presented before those who stand at the head. In other words, I have no right to raise my hand in opposition to a man who is appointed to any position in this Church, simply because I may not like him, or because of some personal disagreement or feeling I may have, but only on the grounds that he is guilty of wrong doing, of transgression of the laws of the Church which would disqualify him for the position which he is called to hold. (In Conference Report, June 1919, p. 92.)

The general membership of the Church does not have the right to nominate individuals for positions of leadership. This power rests with the individual or governing body that has the appropriate stewardship. In the case of selecting an apostle, this responsibility rests with the senior apostle, with the concurrence of his apostolic associates. In selecting the President of the Church, the nominating power rests with the Quorum of the Twelve.

President J. Reuben Clark, Jr., noted that "the sustaining or electing power rests in the body of the Church, which under no circumstances nominates officers, the function of the Church body being solely to sustain or to elect." President Clark went on to say that this system allows for "no electioneering, no speech-making, . . . no proposing of candidates." (In Conference Report, Apr. 1940, pp. 71–72.)

President Spencer W. Kimball observed that "the pattern divine allows for no errors, no conflicts, no ambitions, no ulterior motives. The Lord has reserved for himself the calling of his leaders over his Church." (In Conference Report, Oct. 1972, p. 28.)

The Senior Apostle Exercises the Keys

Although the keys of the kingdom are conferred upon each member of the Quorum of the Twelve Apostles, only the senior apostle exercises them in their fullness at a given time. One of the early leaders of the Church, Elder George Q. Cannon, explained: "Any one of [the Twelve], should an emergency arise, can act as President of the Church, with all the powers, with all the authority, with all the keys, and with every endowment necessary to obtain revelation from God, and to lead and guide this people in the path that leads to the celestial glory; but there is only one man at a time who can hold the keys, who can dictate, who can guide, who can give revelation to the Church. The rest must acquiesce in his action, the rest must be governed by his counsels, the rest must receive his doctrines." (*Journal of Discourses*, 19:234.)

More recently, Elder Bruce R. McConkie added his witness of this principle:

> These keys, having first been revealed from heaven, are given by the spirit of revelation to each man who is both ordained an Apostle and set apart as a member of the Council of the Twelve.
>
> But since keys are the right of presidency, they can only be exercised in their fulness by one man on earth at a time. He is always the senior Apostle, the presiding Apostle, the presiding high priest, the presiding elder. He alone can give direction to all others, direction from which none is exempt.
>
> Thus, the keys, though vested in all of the Twelve, are used by any one of them to a limited degree only, unless and until one of them attains that seniority which makes him the Lord's anointed on earth. ("The Keys of the Kingdom," p. 23.)

President Joseph Fielding Smith noted that when an apostle becomes the presiding officer of the Church, he does not receive any additional authority:

> The Prophet [Joseph Smith], in anticipation of his death, conferred upon the Twelve all the keys and authorities which he held. He did not bestow the keys on

any one member, but upon them *all,* so that *each held the keys* and authorities. All members of the Council of the Twelve since that day have also been given all of these keys and powers. But these powers cannot be exercised by any one of them *until,* if the occasion arises, he is called to be the *presiding officer* of the Church. The Twelve, therefore, in the setting apart of the President do not give him any additional priesthood, but *confirm* upon him that which he has *already* received; they *set him apart* to the office, which it is their right to do. (*Doctrines of Salvation,* 3:155.)

The Senior Apostle Is the Presiding Officer

The senior apostle is the presiding officer or authority of the Church. Where a First Presidency has been organized, the senior apostle has always been the President of the Church. When he dies, thus dissolving the First Presidency, the presiding authority passes to the next senior apostle in the line of succession.

In a letter dated March 28, 1887, President Wilford Woodruff explained: "When the President of the Church dies, who then is the Presiding Authority of the Church? It is the Quorum of the Twelve Apostles (ordained and organized by the revelations of God and none else). Then while these Twelve Apostles preside over the Church, who is the President of the Church[?] It is the President of the Twelve Apostles. And he is virtually as much the President of the Church while presiding over Twelve men as he is when organized as the Presidency of the Church, and presiding over two men." (In Conference Report, Apr. 1970, p. 124.)

President Harold B. Lee reaffirmed this principle: "Immediately following the death of a President, the next ranking body, the Quorum of the Twelve Apostles, becomes the presiding authority, with the President of the Twelve automatically becoming the acting President of the Church until a

President of the Church is officially ordained and sustained in his office." ("The Day in Which We Live," p. 28.)

Is the senior apostle, then, always selected as President? That question has occasionally been raised. In the earlier days of the Church, there were even some among the presiding authorities who raised the question.

In 1880, for example, Elder Orson Pratt suggested that "a young man" should be considered as President of the Church rather than one of the elderly Brethren of the Quorum of the Twelve. This was not the first time such a suggestion had been set forth, for in 1877 Daniel H. Wells, who had served as second counselor to Brigham Young, proposed that thirty-nine-year-old Joseph F. Smith be considered for the presiding office. Elder Heber J. Grant made a similar proposal ten years later. The Quorum of the Twelve disapproved each of these suggestions. (See "The Mormon Succession Crisis," p. 220.)

President Wilford Woodruff once responded to the following question: "Do you know of any reason in case of the death of the President of the Church why the Twelve Apostles should not choose some other person than the president of the Twelve to be the President of the Church?" President Woodruff forthrightly replied:

> I know several reasons why he should not. First, . . . if [he was] not fit to preside over the Church [he was] not fit to preside over the Twelve Apostles. Second, in case of the death of the President of the Church it takes the majority of the Twelve Apostles to appoint the President of the Church, and it is very unreasonable to suppose that the majority of that Quorum could be converted to depart from *the course marked out by inspiration* and followed by the Apostles at the death of Christ and by the Twelve Apostles at the death of Joseph Smith. I see no reason for discussing this subject

until there is some reason for it. (In *Wilford Woodruff,* p. 561; italics added.)

Many years later, President Joseph Fielding Smith, who as one of the Twelve had participated in the transition of the presidency on four previous occasions, declared: "There is no mystery about the choosing of the successor to the President of the Church. The Lord settled this a long time ago, and *the senior apostle automatically becomes the presiding officer of the Church." (Doctrines of Salvation,* 3:156.)

In 1967, while I was teaching the principle of succession to a group of graduate students in Southern California, one of them challenged the above statement by President Smith. At the time Joseph Fielding Smith was the President of the Quorum of the Twelve, second in seniority to David O. McKay, who was serving as President of the Church. The student glibly commented that President Smith's statement was self-serving because he was next in apostolic seniority and that he was "too old" and "too dogmatic in doctrine" to ever become the President. I pointed out that President Smith had made the statement long before he became the number-two apostle, but I did not dissuade the student.

In those days it was appropriate to write directly to one of the General Authorities in seeking answers to questions, and I decided to ask Elder Harold B. Lee, the ranking apostle behind Presidents McKay and Smith, to respond to the question of succession by seniority. I wrote that I did not question the order of succession but felt that having the opinion of another member of the Twelve on the matter would be helpful to my students. Elder Lee was very gracious in responding. A copy of his letter, dated January 19, 1968, follows:

> Dear Brother Brewster:
> I will attempt to answer your question as I have understood it from the brethren much older than I in

experience and in seniority in the presiding councils of the Church.

The Lord in the Doctrine and Covenants 107, speaks of the Quorum of the First Presidency consisting of three presiding high priests, the traveling high council or Quorum of Twelve Apostles, and the First Quorum of Seventy as being equal in authority. This does not mean that they are co-equal, but in the event of the death of the president of the Church when the First Presidency would become disorganized, the Quorum of the Twelve Apostles would then automatically become the acting presiding authority of the Church. Should there ever be an occasion when all of the First Presidency and Quorum of the Twelve were to be taken away by some calamity, the First Quorum of the Seventy would be fully organized and they then by the direction of the Lord could proceed to organize the Church in all its departments.

When the Quorum of the Twelve Apostles become the acting presiding authority upon the death of the president of the Church, the president of the Quorum of the Twelve automatically becomes the acting presiding authority of that body, which means the acting president of the Church until the president of the Church is chosen.

Referring to Section 107, Doctrine and Covenants, it speaks of the President of the Church "chosen by the body and upheld by the faith and prayers of the saints," which has been interpreted to mean president of the Church chosen by the Quorum of Twelve Apostles and sustained by the vote of the membership of the Church, could then preside over the Church. Every member of the Twelve and First Presidency are sustained as prophets, seers and revelators, which means that each such one when ordained as Apostles hold the priesthood necessary to hold every position in the Church if "chosen by the body and upheld by the vote of the Church." This, however, must not be misunderstood. The brethren have declared time and time again, that the only way that one other than the president of the Twelve could be the president of the Church would be that the president of the Twelve would receive a revelation from the Lord designating someone else to act in his stead. That, I firmly believe. It has always been so and in my judgment it will always continue to be so that the President of the Quorum of the Twelve would become the President of the Church unless the Lord were to direct him otherwise.

Trusting that these comments will give you what I understand to be the teaching of the brethren over the years, I am

Sincerely yours,
Harold B. Lee

It is inconceivable that the Lord would ever select one other than His senior apostle to preside over His earthly church. President Spencer W. Kimball's pertinent statement is repeated: "Since the death of his servants is in the power and control of the Lord, *he permits to come to the first place only the one who is destined to take that leadership.* Death and life become the controlling factors." (In Conference Report, Oct. 1972, p. 29; italics added.)

Chapter 7

Apostasy and False Prophets in the Latter Days

Beware of False Spirits and Prophets

One of the great tragedies of life is the loss of individuals who are kept from the truth, or who stray from the strait and narrow path, because they are deceived by false spirits or evil and designing mortals who teach and practice false and damnable doctrines. Through His prophet, the Lord declared that many are "blinded by the subtle craftiness of men, whereby they lie in wait to deceive." (D&C 123:12.)

This spiritual blindness prevents people from seeing or recognizing the truth. Unfortunately, many of those who are blinded or wayward come to believe that the perilous path they are pursuing is the right one. The Prophet Joseph Smith warned that "nothing is a greater injury to the children of men than to be under the influence of a false spirit when they think they have the Spirit of God." (*History of the Church,* 4:573.)

The voices of false spirits are not confined to those unembodied hosts of hell from the largely unseen world of spirits who are in league with the devil, having been cast out of God's presence in the beginning. (See D&C 29:36–38.) False spirits, or false voices, also emanate from "false brethren" (D&C 122:5; 2 Cor. 11:26), "false teachers" (2 Ne. 28:12), "false prophets" (Matt. 7:15), and even "false Christs" (Matt. 24:24). Each of these false voices, whether spirit or mortal, leads people astray.

It was revealed to Brigham Young that "if the people did not receive the spirit of revelation that God had sent for the salvation of the world, they would receive false spirits, and would have revelation" from the powers of darkness. (*Journal of Discourses,* 13:280–81). On the other hand, the Lord declared that "they that are wise and have received the truth, and have taken the Holy Spirit for their guide . . . have not been deceived." (D&C 45:57.)

The Trickery of the Tempter

The devil is the master deceiver. (See Rev. 12:9.) He is the tempter (see Matt. 4:3), the "father of all lies" (2 Ne. 2:18; Moses 4:4), and was a "liar from the beginning" (D&C 93:25). He will use trickery of any kind to lead mankind astray. He will even quote scripture to accomplish his nefarious schemes. (See Matt. 4:6.)

One of the tempter's most effective ploys is to teach some truths or partial truths in order to get an unsuspecting victim to accept one or more falsehoods. It doesn't matter how many truths one may accept if the devil can deceive an individual into accepting one falsehood that puts his or her soul at risk.

On one occasion Elder Orson Pratt was striving to teach this to some members of the Church who had been led astray. They couldn't understand how they could be deceived if they believed in essentially the same things the Church taught. They claimed their beliefs were similar to those espoused by the Church, with just a few exceptions. (The exceptions were the reason they had joined an organization separate from the Church.)

Elder Pratt explained:

> Don't you know that the devil would be very foolish, if he wished to lead astray men who had been in this Church, who had been taught for years to believe the principles you believe in, if he should undertake to lead them astray by telling them there was no truth in all these things? The devil can adapt himself to the belief of any person. If you believed in plurality [of wives] he would make you think it was all right. If he could get you to swallow down one or two great lies that would effect your destruction, and which you would preach and destroy many others, he would not mind how many truths you might believe. He would be willing that you should believe a great many things absolutely true if he could only deceive you and lead you astray and get you to reject some of the fundamental principles of your salvation, and the salvation of the people. (*Journal of Discourses,* 13:73.)

What these misled people did not understand is that believing or accepting even *one* exception to the truths, saving principles, and ordinances of the gospel of Jesus Christ—just one deviation—can lead one out of God's kingdom.

One Can Discern between True and False Prophets

Wherever true prophets of God have been, the devil has brought forth his false prophets. From the day that Lucifer disguised himself and sought to deceive our first parents in the Garden of Eden, he and his evil emissaries have sought to pass themselves off as true messengers of God in order to lead God's children astray.

The Apostle Paul warned of such instances: "For such are false apostles, deceitful workers, transforming themselves into the apostles of Christ. And no marvel; for Satan himself is transformed into an angel of light. Therefore it is no great thing if his ministers also be transformed as the ministers of righteousness; whose end shall be according to their works." (2 Cor. 11:13–15.)

While there are instances in which the adversary is spoken of as posing as an "angel of light" (2 Cor. 11:14; D&C 128:20; 129:8; *Teachings of Joseph Smith,* pp. 162, 214), it appears that these deceitful efforts can be detected by the spiritually discerning. Moses, for example, discerned Satan as a false angel of light: "Where is thy glory," he asked, "for it is *darkness* unto me?" (Moses 1:12–15; italics added.) Perhaps this is why an ancient prophet declared that the devil "transformeth himself *nigh* unto an angel of light." (2 Ne. 9:9; italics added.)

There is a difference in the countenance of a true messenger from God and that of one who is not. Indeed, the words of the prophet Isaiah are very revealing in this respect: "The shew of their countenance doth witness against them," he declared. (Isa. 3:9; 2 Ne. 13:9.) True servants of God will emanate a spirit that is edifying, peaceful, and full of light. Their message will not be contentious, although it may have a disquieting effect on one in need of repentance. In a similar fashion, the listener who is in tune with the Spirit of God, who is humble, prayerful, and striving to live a righteous life, will be edified and know the truthfulness of the message spoken by one truly sent by God.

The Lord gave the following counsel on this matter:

> He that is ordained of me and sent forth to preach the word of truth by the Comforter, in the Spirit of truth, doth he preach it by the Spirit of truth or some other way? And if it be by some other way it is not of God. And again, he that receiveth the word of truth, doth he

121

receive it by the Spirit of truth or some other way? If it be some other way it is not of God.

Therefore, why is it that ye cannot understand and know, that he that receiveth the word by the Spirit of truth receiveth it as it is preached by the Spirit of truth? Wherefore, he that preacheth and he that receiveth, understand one another, and both are edified and rejoice together. And that which doth not edify is not of God, and is darkness. That which is of God is light; and he that receiveth light, and continueth in God, receiveth more light; and that light groweth brighter and brighter until the perfect day. And again, verily I say unto you, and I say it that you may know the truth, that you may chase darkness from among you. (D&C 50:17–25.)

Discerning between Having and Losing the Spirit

One means of discerning between messengers and messages of light and darkness is to consider the spirit in which the message is presented. *As already mentioned, messengers who come from God will not be contentious.* The message they bring will have a calming, spiritually soothing, and peaceful effect upon the listener; unless, of course, one's conscience needs to be pricked, troubled, or seared. The unrepentant will always be uncomfortable when called to repentance. If acted upon positively, however, that discomfort can *turn* one to the Lord. Consider the remarkable example of Alma, whose repentance turned "torment" to "exquisite joy." (See Alma 36.)

The peaceful nature of the Spirit emanating from God's presence, or one who is filled with his Spirit, is illustrated in an experience that Brigham Young had in February of 1847. President Young described a dream or vision in which Joseph Smith appeared to him. In the course of that experience, the Prophet Joseph gave his faithful friend and associate in the ministry the following counsel to carry to the people:

Tell the people to be humble and faithful, and to be sure to keep the spirit of the Lord and it will lead them right. Be careful and not turn away the still small voice; it will teach them what to do and where to go; it will yield the fruits of the kingdom. Tell the Brethren to keep their hearts open to conviction, so that when the Holy Ghost comes to them, their hearts will be ready to receive it. *They can tell the Spirit of the Lord from all other spirits; it will whisper peace and joy to their souls; it will take malice, hatred, strife and all evil from their hearts* and their whole desire will be to do good, bring forth righteousness and build up the kingdom of God. (Manuscript History of Brigham Young: 1846–47, Historical Department, The Church of Jesus Christ of Latter-day Saints, pp. 528–31; italics added; see also Conference Report, Apr. 1989, p. 42.)

On the other hand, darkness is chased away by righteousness. One cannot be successful in obtaining and keeping the Spirit if his or her life is not in order. The Holy Ghost will not abide in the presence of one who is violating God's laws. To turn from God, even ever so slightly, is to turn from light to darkness. Unrepented of, such a turning away leads down the path of apostasy.

President Joseph Fielding Smith warned that "apostasy comes through the sins of omission as well as through sins of commission." For example, failure to take seriously the covenants made at baptism and renewed in the weekly sacrament service can lead one out of the light. One who becomes casual about participating in Sunday worship services, neglectful of regular scripture study and prayer, tolerant of inappropriate media, language, or behavior, and lax in fulfilling Church and family responsibilities puts his or her spiritual well-being at risk. President Smith further noted that "apostasy does not come upon an individual suddenly, but it is a gradual growth in which darkness through sin crowds out the spirit of light from the soul." (*Church History and Modern Revelation,* 2:125.)

The Danger of Being Critical of the Lord's Anointed

One of the quickest ways to lose the Spirit of God and slide into apostasy is to criticize the Lord's anointed. The Prophet Joseph Smith proclaimed that one "who rises up to condemn others, finding fault with the Church, saying that they are out of the way, while he himself is righteous, then know assuredly, that that man is in the high road to apostasy; and if he does not repent, will apostatize, as God lives." (*Teachings of Joseph Smith,* pp. 156–57.)

In 1896, President George Q. Cannon warned of the consequences that follow criticism of the Lord's anointed: "God has chosen His servants. He claims it as His prerogative to condemn them, if they need condemnation. He has not given it to us individually to censure and condemn them. No man, however strong he may be in the faith, however high in the Priesthood, can speak evil of the Lord's anointed and find fault with God's authority on the earth without incurring His displeasure. The Holy Spirit will withdraw itself from such a man, and he will go into darkness." (*Gospel Truth,* 1:278.)

Consider the classic, yet tragic, example of a man who at one time had been the President of the Quorum of the Twelve Apostles. Thomas B. Marsh was excommunicated four years after he was ordained to the holy apostleship. How could one in such a high calling fall away? In 1857, a repentant Thomas B. Marsh returned to the Church and answered this question:

> I have frequently wanted to know how my apostasy began, and I have come to the conclusion that I must have lost the Spirit out of my heart.
>
> The next question is, "How and when did you lose the Spirit?" I became jealous of the Prophet, and then

I saw double, and overlooked everything that was right, and spent all my time in looking for the evil; and then, when the Devil began to lead me, it was easy for the carnal mind to rise up, which is anger, jealousy, and wrath. I could feel it within me; I felt angry and wrathful; and the Spirit of the Lord being gone, as the Scriptures say, I was blinded, and I thought I saw a beam in brother Joseph's eye, but it was nothing but a mote, and my own eye was filled with the beam. (*Journal of Discourses,* 5:206–7.)

Contrast Elder Marsh's tragic experience and the attitude that led to his apostasy with an experience of Brigham Young, the man who succeeded him as the President of the Quorum of Twelve. On one occasion Elder Young admitted that he had once felt critical of the Prophet, but that he quickly dismissed the thought from his mind:

Once in my life, I felt a want of confidence in brother Joseph Smith, soon after I became acquainted with him. It was not concerning religious matters—it was not about his revelations—but it was in relation to his financiering—to his managing the temporal affairs which he undertook. A feeling came over me that Joseph was not right in his financial management, though I presume the feeling did not last sixty seconds, and perhaps not thirty. But that feeling came on me once and once only, from the time I first knew him to the day of his death. It gave me sorrow of heart, and I clearly saw and understood, by the spirit of revelation manifested to me, that if I was to harbor a thought in my heart that Joseph could be wrong in anything, I would begin to lose confidence in him, and that feeling would grow from step to step, and from one degree to another, until at last I would have the same lack of confidence in his being the mouthpiece for the Almighty. . . .

125

I repented of my unbelief, and that too, very suddenly; I repented about as quickly as I committed the error. It was not for me to question whether Joseph was dictated by the Lord at all times and under all circumstances or not. . . .

It was not my prerogative to call him in question with regard to any act of his life. He was God's servant, and not mine. He did not belong to the people but to the Lord, and was doing the work of the Lord. (*Journal of Discourses,* 4:297.)

In recent years, a counselor in the First Presidency has reiterated the need of sustaining the servants of God and of the dangers of finding fault with the Lord's leaders. In a general priesthood meeting in 1974, President N. Eldon Tanner said:

As in the past, there are still some who question the procedure and the choice of the president, and one in particular has written expressing his feeling that he himself should be the president of the Church, but let me remind you that the procedures of the Church and the teachings of Jesus Christ are not on trial. We as individuals are on trial, and have the great privilege and responsibility and blessing of being members of his church and kingdom, and of approving and sustaining the prophet, and it is up to us to prove ourselves worthy of the membership and priesthood which we hold.

Let us always remember that leaders of the Church are responsible to the Lord, and it is for him to straighten them out if they go wrong and to release them when they have finished their mission. We have been warned and forewarned that if we raise ourselves against the authority which God has placed in the Church for its government, unless we repent, he will withdraw his Spirit from us.

Brethren, if we wish to be guided by the Spirit of the Lord and enjoy his blessings, we must be true to the one who has been chosen as our leader and never murmur, complain, or find fault, or feel that someone else should be in his position. ("Chosen of the Lord," *Ensign,* May 1974, p. 85.)

In addition to the perils of being personally critical of the Lord's servants, there is great danger in listening to the voices of critics. Not only will self-appointed judges criticize the leaders of the Lord's kingdom, but they will also find fault with divine doctrines, sacred ordinances, and holy places and practices. Some of these critical voices are spiritually shrill and are easily detected as disturbing and deceptive. However, other voices are more subtle and, almost siren-like, will carefully lead the curious or the unwary into dangerous waters and potential disaster on the reefs of doubt and apostasy.

The spiritually wise will avoid the critics and rely upon the scriptures and the words of the prophets. "For they that are wise and have received the truth," declared the Lord, "have taken the Holy Spirit for their guide, and have not been deceived." (D&C 45:57.) Faith is neither developed nor maintained by spending time listening to or reading the words of detractors. Elder Neal A. Maxwell noted that to study the Church only through the eyes of critics is like interviewing Judas to understand Jesus. ("All Hell Is Moved," in *1977 Devotional Speeches of the Year* [Provo: Brigham Young University Press, 1978], p. 177.)

Revelation Comes through Proper Channels

As pointed out in chapter 1, the Lord reveals His will and directs His church through leaders whom He has called. The Church of Jesus Christ of Latter-day Saints is led by revelation. While each member of the Church has the right to receive revelation for his or her individual needs and stewardship, revelation for the Church as a whole, or any of its units, must come through the designated presiding authority. In 1883 President Joseph F. Smith gave the following counsel:

It is the right of individuals to be inspired and to receive manifestations of the Holy Spirit for their personal guidance, to strengthen their faith, and to encourage them in works of righteousness, in being faithful and observing and keeping the commandments which God has given unto them; it is the privilege of every man and woman to receive revelation to this end, but not further. . . . We can accept nothing as authoritative but that which comes directly through the appointed channel, the constituted organizations of the Priesthood, which is the channel that God has appointed through which to make known His mind and will to the world. (*Journal of Discourses,* 24:188–89.)

President Smith then added this caution:

The moment that individuals look to any other source, that moment they throw themselves open to the seductive influences of Satan, and render themselves liable to become servants of the devil; they lose sight of the true order through which the blessings of the Priesthood are to be enjoyed; they step outside of the pale of the kingdom of God, and are on dangerous ground. Whenever you see a man rise up claiming to have received direct revelation from the Lord to the Church, independent of the order and channel of the Priesthood, you may set him down as an impostor. (*Journal of Discourses,* 24:189–90.)

The Prophet Joseph Smith said, "It is contrary to the economy of God for . . . any one, to receive instruction for those in authority, higher than themselves." Then he added this caution: "Therefore you will see the impropriety of giving heed to them." He then noted that "if any person have a vision or a visitation from a heavenly messenger [or might we say any form of revelation], it must be for his own benefit and instruction." (*Teachings of Joseph Smith,* p. 21.)

Elder Boyd K. Packer added this observation: "In the pattern of constituted authority in the Church we always know where revelation comes from. Revelation is always vertical. There is no horizontal revelation in the Church. It is all vertical. A bishop will get no revelation from a fellow bishop, or a stake president from a fellow stake president; but a bishop will receive it from his stake president, and his stake president from the general officers of the Church." ("Follow the Rule," in *1977 Devotional Speeches of the Year* [Provo: Brigham Young University, 1978], p. 19.)

Some years ago while I was teaching at an institute of religion adjacent to a large university, a man whom I did not know came into my office with a question. He asked, "Is it possible for a heavenly messenger or a translated being such as John the Beloved to visit a lay member of the Church?"

I answered that if God had a purpose in sending such a messenger to mortal man, it surely seemed within the realm of possibility. "Why do you ask?" I inquired.

The man then said, "I have a friend who claims that he was visited by John the Beloved. He says that he knows the messenger was sent from God because he put him to the test outlined in the Doctrine and Covenants. [See D&C 129:1–9.] According to the test, my friend requested the messenger to shake hands with him. They shook hands, and my friend says he felt the flesh. Now, don't you agree this messenger was sent by God?"

I responded with a question: "Why did this messenger visit your friend? Did he have a message for him, and if so what was it?"

My visitor said that the messenger had given his friend a

message to take to the President of the Church, whereupon I immediately said, "It was not of God!" I then explained to the man that it is contrary to the order of heaven for one to receive revelation for someone higher in authority.

"Why did my friend then feel the flesh of the messenger?" the man replied.

I told him that while we may not know the full answer to that question, there were several possibilities to consider: (1) his friend was lying; (2) his friend had dreamed that the occurrence took place; or (3) he had been the object of some hoax foisted on him by some miscreant mortals. "However," I continued, "I know with absolute certainty that your friend was not visited by the Apostle John or any other messenger sent from the presence of God. The story is inconsistent with revealed truth."

President Harold B. Lee stated that "the President of the Church . . . alone has the right to declare new doctrine. . . . The President of the Church alone may declare the mind and will of God to His people. No officer nor any other church in the world has this high and lofty prerogative." (*Stand Ye in Holy Places* [Salt Lake City: Deseret Book, 1974], p. 110.) The President of the Church is the only one who may receive revelation for the entire Church or for himself. While the Prophet works closely with trusted counselors and associates in the Quorum of the Twelve Apostles, listening to and not infrequently following the counsel they give, he is not led by revelation given through another. The Prophet's file leader is the Lord Himself--He who is the head of the Church.

A First Presidency Declaration

Because there have always been those who are deceived, and the deceivers and the deceived are still among us today, it is worthwhile to reproduce an official declaration of the First Presidency issued on August 2, 1913, entitled "A Warning Voice":

From the days of Hiram Page [D&C 28], at different periods there have been manifestations from delusive spirits to members of the Church. Sometimes these have come to men and women who because of transgression became easy prey to the Arch-Deceiver. At other times people who pride themselves on their strict observance of the rules and ordinances and ceremonies of the Church are led astray by false spirits, who exercise an influence so imitative of that which proceeds from a Divine source that even these persons, who think they are "the very elect," find it difficult to discern the essential difference. Satan himself has transformed himself to be apparently "an angel of light."

When visions, dreams, tongues, prophecy, impressions or any extraordinary gift or inspiration conveys something out of harmony with the accepted revelations of the Church or contrary to the decisions of its constituted authorities, Latter-day Saints may know that it is not of God, no matter how plausible it may appear. Also they should understand that directions for the guidance of the Church will come, by revelation, through the head. All faithful members are entitled to the inspiration of the Holy Spirit for themselves, their families, and for those over whom they are appointed and ordained to preside. But anything at discord with that which comes from God through the head of the Church is not to be received as authoritative or reliable. In secular as well as spiritual affairs, Saints may receive Divine guidance and revelation affecting themselves, but this does not convey authority to direct others, and is not to be accepted when contrary to Church covenants, doctrine or discipline, or to known facts, demonstrated truths, or good common sense. No person has the right to induce his fellow members of the Church to engage in speculations or take stock in ventures of any kind on the specious claim of Divine revelation or vision or dream, especially when it is in opposition to the voice of recognized authority, local or general. The Lord's Church "is a house of order." It is not governed by individual gifts or manifestations, but by the order and power of the Holy Priesthood as sustained by the voice and vote of the Church in its appointed conferences.

The history of the Church records many pretended revelations claimed by impostors or zealots who believed in the manifestations they sought to lead other persons to accept, and in every instance, disappointment, sorrow and disaster have resulted therefrom. Financial loss and sometimes utter ruin have followed. We feel it our duty to warn the Latter-day Saints against fake mining schemes which have no warrant for success beyond the professed spiritual manifestations of their projectors and the influence gained over the excited minds of their victims. We caution the Saints against investing money or property in shares of stock which bring no profit to anyone but those who issue and trade in them. Fanciful schemes to make money for the alleged purpose of "redeeming Zion" or providing means for "the salvation of the dead" or other seemingly worthy objects, should not deceive anyone acquainted with the order of the Church, and will result only in waste of time and labor, which might be devoted now to doing something tangible and worthy and of record on earth and in heaven.

Be not led by any spirit or influence that discredits established authority, contradicts true scientific principles and discoveries, or leads away from the direct revelations of God for the government of the Church. *The Holy Ghost does not contradict its own revealings.* Truth is always harmonious with itself. Piety is often the cloak of error. The counsels of the Lord through the channel he has appointed will be followed with safety.

Therefore, O! ye Latter-day Saints, profit by these words of warning. (Signed by Joseph F. Smith, Anthon H. Lund, and Charles W. Penrose of the First Presidency; in James R. Clark, *Messages of the First Presidency,* 6 vols. [Salt Lake City: Bookcraft, 1965–75], 4:285–86; italics added.)

Avoid Alternate Voices

Almost a century later, this inspired counsel by the First Presidency is still pertinent. In our day we are still troubled by individuals who rise up with false revelations, claiming a higher authority than that possessed by the one whom God has designated to lead His church. We still have some of "the elect" being led astray and destroyed, spiritually and temporally, as modern-day deceivers peddle their pernicious promises and damning doctrines.

Latter-day Saints would do well to follow the example of an earlier people of great faith—the people of Ammon. In contrast to their foolish Nephite neighbors whose hearts were led away the preachings of a purveyor of false doctrine, the people of Ammon "were more wise." (Alma 30:20.) When the false prophet Korihor came among them, they did not waste their time in listening to his malevolent message. Their faith was secure. They took the antichrist to their high priest, who then removed him from their presence. (See Alma 30:18–21.)

In like manner, the followers of Christ today would be wise to avoid wasting their time listening to, or reading the words of, those who do not preach "sound doctrine." (See 2 Tim. 4:3–4.) A modern-day apostle, Elder Dallin H. Oaks, has cautioned us against "alternate voices." These are those who speak "without calling or authority." While some may be well-meaning, others' "avowed or secret object is to deceive and devour the flock." ("Alternate Voices," *Ensign,* May 1989, pp. 27–30.)

Latter-day Saints are best served by searching the scriptures and following the counsel of God's living prophet — the President of The Church of Jesus Christ of Latter-day Saints. He is the one whom the Lord has declared holds the keys of priesthood authority, and "there is never but one on the earth at a time on whom this power and the keys of this priesthood are conferred." (D&C 132:7.)

Chapter 8

Follow the Living Prophet

The Lord's Prophet

As initially witnessed in chapter one and repeated throughout this book, the President of The Church of Jesus Christ of Latter-day Saints is the prophet, seer, and revelator of the Lord on the earth today. He is the one through whom God reveals His will to mankind. He is the one who holds all priesthood keys available to mankind and who, therefore, authorizes all ordinances of the gospel.

Members of The Church of Jesus Christ of Latter-day Saints bear this testimony to the world, for it is absolutely vital to the salvation of every man, woman, and child of accountability to gain a personal witness of God's prophet. Such a testimony does not denigrate the position of the Lord Jesus Christ as our Savior, "for there is none other name under heaven given among men, whereby we must be saved" than that of our Redeemer. (Acts 4:12; see also 2 Ne. 25:20.) However, through his prophet and those who serve under his direction, the Lord authorizes the ordinances and covenants that lead to salvation.

At the beginning of this last dispensation of the gospel

of Jesus Christ, the Savior himself declared: "The arm of the Lord shall be revealed; and the day cometh that they who will not hear the voice of the Lord, neither the voice of his servants, neither *give heed to the words of the prophets and apostles,* shall be cut off from among the people." (D&C 1:14; italics added.)

The prophet and President of The Church of Jesus Christ of Latter-day Saints is the senior apostle on earth today, holding the same keys of authority that Christ's chief apostle, Peter, held two centuries ago. Peter himself, along with his two apostolic associates, James and John, helped restore the keys of priesthood authority to the earth in our day. (See D&C 27:12–13; 128:20.)

The significance of accepting both Jesus Christ and his prophets was declared by the First Presidency in 1935:

> Two great truths must be accepted by mankind if they shall save themselves: first, that Jesus is the Christ, the Messiah, the Only Begotten, the very Son of God, whose atoning blood and resurrection save us from the physical and spiritual death brought to us by the Fall; and next, that God has again restored to the earth, in these last days, through the Prophet Joseph [Smith], His holy Priesthood with the fulness of the everlasting Gospel, for the salvation of all men on the earth. Without these truths man may not hope for the riches of the life hereafter. (Heber J. Grant, J. Reuben Clark, David O. McKay, "A Testimony to the World," *Improvement Era,* Apr. 1935, p. 205.)

Living Prophets and Deceased Prophets

One of the difficulties mankind seems to have always had is in making the transition from following a prophet who is deceased to following the living one who has taken the former prophet's place. Perhaps the people are accustomed to the ways and words of the former prophet, or perhaps they have mistakenly placed their loyalty in the man rather than in the mantle of authority he wears. Whatever the reason, there have been those who have stumbled and faltered in their faith whenever such transitions have taken place.

During the meridian of time, the Savior was rejected by some because they claimed to be "Moses' disciples." (John 9:28.) Others placed their undying allegiance on Abraham: "Art thou greater than our father Abraham?" they cried in their rejection of the Son of God. (John 8:53.) In their twisted thinking, these blind loyalists to the past thought they did not need any other prophet; not even the *Holy One* to whom Moses and Abraham gave their loyalty and worshipful obedience, for the Jesus of the New Testament was the same who was Jehovah of the Old Testament—a God come to earth.

Latter-day Saints have not been immune to the problem of misplaced loyalties. Some Church members have found it difficult to make a transition from one prophet to the next. Elder Spencer W. Kimball noted that "even in the Church many are prone to garnish the sepulchres of yesterday's prophets and mentally stone the living ones." ("To His Servants the Prophets," *Instructor,* Aug. 1960, p. 257.)

Elder Harold B. Lee observed that each time the President of The Church of Jesus Christ of Latter-day Saints dies, some Church members also die spiritually because they are unable to follow the newly called *living* prophet. They are willing "to believe in someone who is dead and gone and accept his authority more than the words of a living authority." ("The Living Prophet," *Instructor,* Aug. 1965, pp. 308–9.)

The Lord's church is a living church, and it requires a living prophet. President Ezra Taft Benson observed that "God's revelations to Adam did not instruct Noah how to build the Ark. Noah needed his own revelation." Each generation requires revelation for the challenges and needs of its day. "Therefore," continued President Benson, "the most important prophet so far as you and I are concerned is the one living in our day and age to whom the Lord is currently revealing His will for us." President Benson cautioned, "Beware of those who would pit the dead prophets against the living prophets, for the living prophets always take precedence." ("Fourteen Fundamentals in Following the Prophet," in *1980 Devotional Speeches of the Year* [Provo: Brigham Young University, 1981], p. 26.)

Living Prophets and the Scriptures

Not only do the living prophets take precedence over those who have gone before them, but their inspired words also have a priority over scripture. When he was a member of the Quorum of the Twelve, President Ezra Taft Benson explained this principle: "Because [the living prophet] gives the word of the Lord for us today, his words have an even more immediate importance than those of the dead prophets. When speaking under the influence of the Holy Ghost his words are scripture. (See D&C 68:4.)" (In Conference Report, Oct. 1963, p. 17.)

Placing a priority on the living prophet does not downgrade the importance of holy writ, for the same God whose words are found in the scriptures is the one who is revealing His mind and will to the living prophet. The scriptures and the words of the living prophet are used in tandem, for "every generation has need of the ancient scripture plus the current scripture from the living prophet," said President Benson. (In Conference Report, Korea Area Conference, 1975, p. 52.) President John Taylor also provided the following explanation of the need for living scripture:

> The Bible is good; and Paul told Timothy to study

it, that he might be a workman that need not be ashamed, and that he might be able to conduct himself aright before the *living* church, the pillar and ground of truth. The church-mark, with Paul, was the foundation, the pillar, the ground of truth, the *living* church, not the dead letter. The Book of Mormon is good, and the Doctrine and Covenants, as land-marks. But a mariner who launches into the ocean requires a more certain criterion. He must be acquainted with heavenly bodies, and take his observations from them, in order to steer his barque aright. Those books are good for example, precedent, and investigation, and for developing certain laws and principles. But they do not, they cannot, touch every case required to be adjudicated and set in order. . . .

We require *a living tree—a living fountain—living intelligence, proceeding from the living priesthood in heaven, through the living priesthood on earth.* . . . And from the time that Adam first received a communication from God, to the time that John, on the Isle of Patmos, received his communication, or Joseph Smith had the heavens opened to him, it always required new revelations, adapted to the peculiar circumstances in which the churches or individuals were placed. (*Gospel Kingdom,* p. 34; italics added.)

The Savior himself stressed the need of living words over long-standing written ones. In an exchange with the detractors of His day, Jesus chided them because they were not abiding by the words of the Father, "for whom he hath sent, him ye believe not." The Savior then chastized them for thinking that they would find eternal life in the scriptures ("in them ye *think* ye have eternal life") while ignoring Him of whom the scriptures testified. "Ye will not come to me, that ye might have life," He admonished. (John 5:38–40; italics added.) In their misdirected loyalty, these people were worshipping the *word* rather than the *Author.*

Elder Orson F. Whitney, who served as an apostle for twenty-five years, provided us the following explanation regarding the need for current revelation:

> The great distinguishing feature that differentiates God's Church from all other churches under the sun — [is] this, that while they are founded upon books and traditions and the precepts of men, this Church is built upon the rock of Christ, upon the principle of immediate and continuous revelation. The Latter-day Saints do not do things because they happen to be printed in a book. They do not do things because God told the Jews to do them; nor do they do or leave undone anything because of instructions that Christ gave to the Nephites. Whatever is done by this Church is because God, speaking from heaven in our day, has commanded this Church to do it. *No book presides over this Church, and no book lies at its foundation.* You cannot pile up books enough to take the place of God's priesthood, inspired by the power of the Holy Ghost. That is the constitution of the Church of Christ. . . . *Divine revelation adapts itself to the circumstances and conditions of men, and change upon change ensues as God's progressive work goes on to its destiny.* There is no book big enough or good enough to preside over this Church. . . .
>
> No man ought to contend for what is in the books, in the face of God's mouthpiece, who speaks for him and interprets his word. To so contend is to defer to the dead letter in prefer[e]nce to the living oracle, which is always a false position. What the Lord said to the Jews and Nephites, two thousand years ago, or what he said to the Latter-day Saints fifty or sixty years ago, has no force whatever at this time, unless it agrees with present-day revelation, with the Lord's most recent instructions to his people through his chosen or appointed servants or servant; and they who ignore this fact are liable to

get into trouble. *It is the latest word from God that must be heeded, in preference to any former revelation,* however true. . . .

God's work is progressive. It changes its appearance, but never its principles. The truths upon which it is founded are eternal, unalterable, but there are many regulations that change and change and change, as the work of God goes on. (In Conference Report, Oct. 1916, pp. 55–56; italics added.)

"The principle of present revelation," said President John Taylor, "is the very foundation of our religion." (*Gospel Kingdom,* p. 35.) God reveals "line upon line, precept upon precept" according to our faith and need to know. (2 Ne. 28:30; see also D&C 98:12; A of F 1:9.)

In the early days of the Lord's latter-day church, one man who did not understand the priority of prophets over scripture cautioned the leaders that they should confine themselves to giving revelations according to what was already found in scripture. President Wilford Woodruff reported what followed:

When he concluded, Brother Joseph [Smith] turned to Brother Brigham Young and said, "Brother Brigham I want you to take the stand and tell us your views with regard to the written [or living] oracles and the written word of God." Brother Brigham took the stand, and he took the Bible, and laid it down; he took the Book of Mormon, and laid it down; and he took the Book of Doctrine and Covenants, and laid it down before him, and he said: "There is the written word of God to us, concerning the work of God from the beginning of the world, almost, to our day." "And now," said he, "when compared with the living oracles those books are nothing to me; those *books do not convey the word of God direct to us now, as do the words of a Prophet* or a man bearing the Holy Priesthood in our day and generation. I would rather have the living oracles than all the writing in the books." That was the course he pursued. When he was through, Brother Joseph said to the congregation: "Brother Brigham has told you the word of the Lord, and he has told you the truth." (In Conference Report, Oct. 1897, pp. 22–23; italics added.)

At another time, President Wilford Woodruff added his own testimony of this principle: "If we had before us every revelation which God ever gave to man; if we had the Book of Enoch; if we had the untranslated plates [of the Book of Mormon] before us in the English language; if we had the records of the Revelator St. John which are sealed up, and all other revelations, and they were piled up here a hundred feet high, the Church and kingdom of God could not grow, in this or any other age of the world, without the living oracles of God." (In *Millennial Star* 51:548.)

Prophets Become More Than Ordinary Men

Some express concern that the prophets of our day appear to be ordinary men. They wonder if their words should really carry the weight of ancient prophets. Forgotten by these skeptics is the fact that the same Lord who spoke anciently to Moses, or the other prophets and apostles, is the one who speaks to the prophets and apostles of our day. Their inspired words come from the same source.

The Lord selects His leaders for His purposes, and the qualifications that these men of God possess may differ from what the world may have expected. In 1951, Elder Spencer W. Kimball said, "I would not say that those leaders whom the Lord chooses are necessarily the most brilliant, nor the most highly trained, but they are the chosen, and when chosen of the Lord they are his recognized authority, and the people who stay close to them have safety." (In Conference Report, Apr. 1951, p. 104.)

More recently, Elder Boyd K. Packer provided the following insights:

> It is not because of travel nor professional success that we ought to pay heed to [God's chosen servants]. Nor is it because they are nimble of mind or wise in years. These things are incidental only.
>
> We listen to them because they have been "called of God, by prophecy, and by the laying on of hands, by those who are in authority to preach the gospel and administer in the ordinances thereof." (Article of Faith 5.)
>
> They are given divine authority. Not one of them aspired to the office he holds, nor did he call himself, for "in the Church of Jesus Christ of Latter-day Saints, one takes the place to which one is duly called," said President [J. Reuben] Clark, "which place one neither seeks or declines." (*Improvement Era,* June 1951, p. 412.) (In Conference Report, Oct. 1968, p. 75.)

In contrast to royal kingdoms on earth where princes and kings are designated from birth and are reared in courts of splendor with the goal of someday having them ascend a throne or occupy a regal position in society, prophets are generally reared among ordinary people, often in humble circumstances. Although prophets come into life with a mission to perform, having been foreordained to their callings, for the most part the Lord keeps this information secret while He quietly but carefully directs His future prophets along their path of preparation. To most of their peers, friends, and acquaintances, these future prophets appear as ordinary boys or men.

Even the Savior appeared to most to be but an ordinary man. Isaiah described Him as having "no form nor comeliness; and when we shall see him, there is no beauty that we should desire him." (Isa. 53:2; see also Mosiah 14:2.) Indeed, the Son of Man was mistakenly seen by His neighbors as *just* "the carpenter's son." (Matt. 13:55.)

The Apostles Peter, James, John, and Andrew were all humble fishermen. While he had more formal training than most of his apostolic associates, Paul was a tentmaker by trade. Each of these great disciples was undoubtedly looked upon as an ordinary man, but that did not change the divine nature of each one's apostolic appointment as a special servant of the Lord.

The leaders whom the Lord has selected to serve Him in our day have come from a variety of backgrounds and occupations. But, counseled Elder Mark E. Petersen, we "must look beyond the former occupations and personal activities of our modern leaders and see them as the servants of God that they are now." Elder Petersen added this observation:

> What if we did know them as boys in the neighborhood and saw no halos about them? What if we did mingle with them as they lived routine and ordinary lives in the past, meeting the world as it came, day by day? We must realize that conditions have changed!
>
> God has now lifted them out of those familiar patterns and has given them a new status in life. He has summoned them to high callings in his ministry. A sacred mantle has descended upon them, the mantle of their divine commission, the mantle of prophecy!
>
> They speak with new voices; they are guided by a heavenly light. *They are ordinary no longer!* They are the anointed ones—the chosen ones—chosen by Almighty God! ("Follow the Prophets," *Ensign*, Nov. 1981, p. 66.)

Those who are prone to myopically focus on the seeming ordinariness of the Lord's anointed, the mortal mistakes of the man, or the physical failings or other limitations of a prophet are in danger of missing the message sent from the Lord. President Spencer W. Kimball once warned the people that "the swiftest method of rejection of the holy prophets has been to find a pretext, however false or absurd, to dismiss the man so that his message could also be dismissed." ("Listen to the Prophets," *Ensign,* May 1978, p. 77.)

The Prophets Will Never Lead Us Astray

Becoming more than an ordinary man does not mean that these leaders have attained perfection. They are still mortals, subject to making mistakes. None has claimed perfection. However, one must not therefore conclude that the prophets will ever preach or teach false doctrines. The Prophet Joseph Smith once told the Saints, "I never told you I was perfect; but *there is no error in the revelations which I have taught.*" (*History of the Church,* 6:366; italics added.) This same statement could be said of each man who has worn the prophet's mantle in this dispensation.

We have the assurance that the prophet who stands at the head of The Church of Jesus Christ of Latter-day Saints will not lead the people astray. Consider the following testimonies:

In 1890, the fourth President of the Church, Wilford Woodruff, declared: "I say to Israel, the Lord will never permit me nor any other man who stands as the President of this Church, to lead you astray. It is not in the programme. It is not in the mind of God. If I were to attempt that, the Lord would remove me out of my place, and so He will any other man who attempts to lead the children of men astray from the oracles of God and from their duty." (In *Wilford Woodruff,* p. 572.)

Speaking as the Lord's prophet in 1972, President Joseph Fielding Smith stated: "I think there is one thing which we should have exceedingly clear in our minds. Neither the President of the Church, nor the First Presidency, nor the united voice of the First Presidency and the Twelve will ever lead the Saints astray or send forth counsel to the world that is contrary to the mind and will of the Lord. An individual may fall by the wayside, or have views, or give counsel which falls short of what the Lord intends. But the voice of the First Presidency and the united voice of those others who hold with them the keys of the kingdom shall always guide the Saints and the world in those paths where the Lord wants them to be." ("Eternal Keys and the Right to Preside," p. 88.)

Another of God's prophets, President Heber J. Grant, provided these testimonies: "You need have no fear . . . that any man will ever stand at the head of the Church of Jesus Christ unless our Heavenly Father wants him to be there." (*Gospel Standards,* p. 68.) "Any Latter-day Saint who thinks for one minute that this Church is going to fail is not a really converted Latter-day Saint. There will be no failure in this Church. It has been established for the last time, never to be given to another people and never to be thrown down." (*Church News,* Oct. 27, 1962, p. C-2; see also Dan. 2:44; D&C 112:30.)

Safety Comes in Obtaining a Testimony of the Living Prophet

At the time The Church of Jesus Christ of Latter-day Saints was organized on April 6, 1830, the Lord commanded the members to follow the prophet whom He had placed over His church: "Wherefore, meaning the church, thou shalt give heed unto all his words and commandments which he shall give unto you as he receiveth them, walking in all holiness before me; for his word ye shall receive, as if from mine own mouth, in all patience and faith." (D&C 21:4–5.)

President Harold B. Lee observed that our "only safety" will come in doing exactly what the Lord said in the revelation just cited. He then noted that "there will be some things that take patience and faith. You may not like what comes from the authority of the Church. It may contradict your political views. It may contradict your social views. It may interfere with some of your social life." But, he cautioned, "Your safety and ours depends upon whether or not we follow the ones whom the Lord has placed to preside over his church. He knows whom he wants to preside over this church, and he will make no mistake." President Lee then admonished all to "keep our eye on the President of the Church." ("Uphold the Hands of the President of the Church," *Improvement Era,* Dec. 1970, p. 127.)

The Lord does not require blind obedience, for He wants each individual to gain his or her own witness of the truth of what the prophets are saying. Twenty years prior to making the above statement, President Lee said: "It is not alone sufficient for us as Latter-day Saints to follow our leaders and to accept their counsel, but we have the greater obligation to gain for ourselves the unshakable testimony of the divine appointment of these men and the witness that what they have told us is the will of our Heavenly Father." (In Conference Report, Oct. 1950, p. 130.)

This places the responsibility for knowing and following the word of the Lord squarely on the shoulders of the individual. The challenge to each man, woman, and child of accountability is to gain a personal witness of the divine nature of a prophet's calling and of the truthfulness of the words he speaks. And then, to follow the counsel given.

We live in a very troubled world. "Where is there safety in the world today?" asked President Harold B. Lee. He then answered by stating, "Safety can't be won by tanks and guns and the airplanes and atomic bombs. There is only one place of safety and that is within the realm of the power of Almighty God that he gives to those who keep his commandments and listen to his voice, as he speaks through the channels that he has ordained for that purpose." (In Conference Report, Oct. 1973, p. 169.)

While no one is guaranteed safety from all physical harm in the world today, there is a safety that is much more significant — spiritual safety or well-being. The inspired counsel of the Lord's prophet — the President of The Church of Jesus Christ of Latter-day Saints — if followed, will lead us safely back to the presence of our Father in Heaven and His Son Jesus Christ.

"When we are instructed by the President of this Church," proclaimed Elder George Albert Smith, "we believe he tells us what the Lord would have us do. To us it is something more than just the advice of man." (In Conference Report, Oct. 1930, p. 66.) The Lord Himself emphasized this principle when He declared, "whether by mine own voice or by the voice of my servants, it is the same." (D&C 1:38.)

Those who reject the words of the living prophet of God place their souls at risk, for, as previously cited, the Lord declared that "they who will not hear the voice of the Lord, neither the voice of his servants, neither give heed to the words of the prophets and apostles, shall be cut off from among the people." (D&C 1:14.) To truly follow Christ is to follow His anointed servants, for they teach what He would have us know and do. We bear witness to the world of the living Christ and of the authority of His living prophet. We invite all mankind to "come unto Christ, and be perfected in him." (Moro. 10:32.)

Index

Index

Woodruff, 85–86; Lorenzo Snow, 86–87; Joseph F. Smith, 87–90; Heber J. Grant, 90–93; George Albert Smith, 93–94; David O. McKay, 94–97; Joseph Fielding Smith, 97–98; Harold B. Lee, 98–99; Spencer W. Kimball, 99–102; Ezra Taft Benson, 102–4; the Lord is in charge, 104–5; nature of apostolic keys, 106–8; apostolic office conferred by those in authority, 108–9; apostles must be sustained, 109–11; senior apostle exercises keys, 111–13; senior apostle is presiding officer, 113–17

Sustaining apostles, 109–11

Talmage, James E., 26
Tanner, N. Eldon, 98, 126–27
Taylor, John, 56, 61, 79–85, 138–39, 141
Teachings of prophets, 10–12
Testimony: of Jesus, 13–15; of apostolic keys, 47–49; of prophet, 135, 146–48
Thompson, Charles, 71–72
Three Witnesses, 35, 39–40
Truth vs. falsehood, 119–20

Visions: First Vision, 16–17; visions of Moroni, 17–19; vision of forces of evil, 18–19; Joseph Smith tutored by heavenly messengers, 19–20; restoration of priesthood keys, 21–23; visions in Kirtland Temple, 24–28; false visions, 57–58, 121–22, 129–31

"Warning Voice, A" 130–33
Wells, Daniel H., 79
Wells, Junius, 70

Whitmer, David, 35–37, 39–40, 68–70
Whiting, Chancey, 62
Whitney, Orson F., 140–41
Widtsoe, John A., 109–10
Wight, Lyman, 65–66
Williams, Frederick G., 34–35
Winder, John R., 90
Woodruff, Wilford: on apostles receiving keys, 47; seniority of, 80–82; as senior apostle, 85–86; on reorganization of First Presidency, 86; on senior apostle being President, 113–15; on contemporary revelation, 141–42; claimed President will never lead Saints astray, 145

Year's supply, 12–13
Young, Brigham: on Joseph Smith's ordination as apostle, 24; on being prophet and president, 29–30; on first apostles of latter days, 39; chosen as apostle, 39–41; on Hyrum Smith, 47; on apostolic keys, 48, 106; debated Sidney Rigdon over Church leadership, 52–55; on apostasy, 75; as senior apostle, 76–79; changed seniority of apostles, 81–84; called Joseph F. Smith and Brigham Young, Jr., to apostleship, 87; on false and true revelation, 119; had vision of Joseph Smith, 122–23; squelched criticism of Joseph Smith, 125–26; on continuing revelation, 141–42
Young, Brigham, Jr., 79, 87–89
Young, John W., 79
Young, Phineas, 40
Young, Richard W., 91–92

Zion's Camp, 35

154